True To Your Core

True to Your Core

Uncovering the Subconscious Beliefs That Wreak Havoc on Your Life

Bonnie Kelly

ISBN-13: 9781537115405
ISBN-10: 1537115405
Library of Congress Control Number: 2016913706
CreateSpace Independent Publishing Platform
North Charleston, South Carolina

Forward

To my father and dearest friend. I have no words to describe my gratitude for all you have taught me. The guidance, lessons, and love you continue to shower upon me shall never be forgotten. Your support has allowed me to rise from the ashes of a lost soul and step into a life where anything is possible.

Thank you for your love. Thank you for your support. And thank you for being you. May this book be a symbol of the many teaching you shared and the love I have for you.

Table of Contents

*Check Out Our **Free** Video Master Series That Accompanies The Homework Outlined In This Book At: www.TrueToYourCore.com*

Introduction: It's Not Your Fault But It Is Your Responsibility

So OFTEN IN life we carry the weight of regret, shame, and guilt of our past. We harbor resentment and anguish over what was. If you remain unaware of the impact your history has on your mind, you allow these hidden shadows of your past to wreak havoc in your present. Even after years of therapy and insight, you can find yourself stuck in a cycle of self-sabotage. These hidden shadows can wreak havoc in relationships, finances and business, while destroying your self-esteem and sense of self-worth. You can be reading this right now and still have no idea how deep the roots of your history have infected your mind. So much energy is wasted blaming, shaming, and complaining about ourselves.

Yet, never once do we stop to wonder, "Is it really all my fault?"

The brain is a mysterious place. In fact, scientists still do not understand the power of our brain in its entirety. What we do understand, however, has changed the way we look at the impact our childhood has on our current emotional well-being and how it affects the way we experience our lives as adults.

If you've read self-help books, attended workshops, been to therapy or talked to a counselor yet *still* find yourself suffering from depression, feeling not good enough or unconsciously sucked into a self-sabotage cycle, then this book is for you.

Many of your best efforts to change may have been focused on transforming the conscious mind. But this isn't where the power lies. The *sub*conscious mind is the silent monster lurking in the shadows and is infinitely more powerful than the conscious mind.

Our childhood experiences shaped, molded and installed subconscious beliefs that act like programs on a computer waiting to be utilized. It is during this installation process prior to our adolescence that we develop our identity. You decide whether you are good enough, how much value you have, and even how you will connect with others. It is also during this time that viruses are unintentionally installed.

These undetected viruses have been undermining your best efforts to change and it's time to finally put an end to their reign.

The first step is to understand how the conscious and subconscious minds work. The conscious mind is where we typically focus. This is our attention and is the part of the brain we use to learn or develop new skills. This part of the brain captures our conscious thoughts and active feelings, but plays only a small role in our day-to-day activities. The powerhouse of the brain lies within the subconscious mind.

The subconscious mind is estimated to control about 80% of what you do on a daily basis, and is the primary motivator behind the majority of your decision making. The secret programs locked deep within this part of your mind can be either constructive or destructive. They will build you up or break you down. Destructive viruses feed off our negative conscious thoughts and experiences gaining strength and momentum to overpower healthy programs. They constantly re-validate the "truth" of their negativity to keep you stuck in a never-ending self-sabotaging cycle.

This painful re-validation process will knock the wind out of your sails leaving you feeling stuck, worthless, hopeless, depressed or like you don't matter. Unless uncovered, these unconscious viruses continue to spread, wreaking havoc in your life and becoming so powerful that this false truth becomes "true" to your core. Regardless of who you are, what you have done, or been through, these viruses are NOT YOUR FAULT. However, once you become aware of their existence, it IS your responsibility to do something about it.

Throughout this book, I'll share my own experience of growing up to illustrate how these negative core beliefs are formed during the formative years of our childhood. I'll use my own real life stories to show you how these viruses, if left unchallenged, can impact your life, decisions, and happiness. And throughout this book, I'll empower you with the tools necessary to install anti-virus software and remove these toxic beliefs once and for all.

A side note from me to you: The stories you are about to read are based on actual events that occurred in my life, however, some of the names and places have been changed. For example, the names, places, and story were modified to conceal the identity of my sexual predator. The real abuser was an extended family member who was never prosecuted for his crimes. To ensure this book and value it brings to you is never pulled from the shelves, I changed the setting and the character to a wealthy family friend named "John."

CHAPTER 1

Where It All Begins

WITH EVERY PASSING hour, my excitement faded. Morning quickly turned into afternoon. It had been hours since lunch and I couldn't take the anticipation any longer. My mother sat at the kitchen table busily working on her craft projects as I approached. I stood anxiously, not knowing how exactly to ask, hoping it wouldn't result in a spanking or, even worse, not being allowed to go. As I hesitated over what to say, my mother muttered, "I told you he didn't care." Overcome by this sad possibility, I silently stood paralyzed.

I felt small and hopeless. What did she mean he didn't care? How couldn't he? What had I done for him to stop caring? For the first time, this ugly train of thought flooded my mind. It'd been months since we'd last seen him. Still, he had to care, he just had to.

Suddenly the sound of roaring thunder filled the room and I quickly snapped back to that moment. My mother erupted from her chair in a fury and bolted through the front door. Confused, I sprinted for the window. A brand new T-Top Firebird rumbled into the driveway, a car that was rare in our neck of the woods. It glistened against the white snow as it came to a roaring stop in front of our house. My mother had just reached the driver's door as the engine cut off and the door swung open. A tall, slender, wild-haired young man stepped out.

"DADDY!" I screamed dashing out onto the front yard, hurling myself toward him. Just shy of leaping into his arms, my excitement came to a sudden halt as my mother turned and intercepted me. Grinning from ear to ear, I swayed from side to side desperately trying to look past my mother for a closer glimpse of my father. Her words were a jumble to me and I heard just a few words, "Go get dressed." I nodded and raced back into the house.

In my excitement, I hadn't noticed I'd run out into the snow with no shoes or a coat. Back inside, my brother and I scrambled to find matching boots and mittens from the winter-clothing bin. We smiled at each other and bundled ourselves up. Rushing back outside, we sensed a heightened tension in the air. But our father quickly brushed past our mother and, falling to his knees, he swept both of us up into his arms. He hugged us in a tight embrace.

"I knew you'd come," I softly whispered. Startled, my father jerked back while still gripping us close. "Of course I would! What would ever give you the idea I wouldn't?" He turned to glare at my mother, who was now accompanied by our stepfather. Turning back to us with a big smile that stretched across his face, my father said, "Are you ready for some fun?!"

"YES!" we both shouted with excitement as we ran to the car.

We spent the rest of the afternoon and evening with loving, laughing people, food and presents. Our father's family had gathered to celebrate the holidays early, since having him home was as rare as having us with them. Within just a few weeks, our father would return to duty at sea, unable to come home for many more months. Smothered with affection and gratitude, the evening flew by in a flash. My brother and I were playing with our new toys in the back room, completely unaware most everyone had gone, when our grandmother popped in. "Who wants ice cream?" she asked in an endearing voice surely no one could refuse.

We enjoyed our Neapolitan ice cream in the kitchen, trading strawberry and vanilla flavors between us without a care in the world. The sound of *Jeopardy!* blared from the living room TV as the phone rang for a second time. Our father grabbed the phone angrily. Within minutes, the peace which once enveloped the house was gone. We could hear our enraged mother yelling through the phone as our father answered with ferocious anger.

"Don't you worry yourselves now, my loves." Our grandmother knelt down between us, her voice soothing the tension. "Go on now, enjoy your ice cream. Everything is going to be alright now, you hear?" We nodded, trying to ignore the yelling in the background. Within minutes, our father slammed the phone down and stormed outside. My older brother shrugged his shoulders. "Must need to cool off," he explained. Sensing the calm in his voice, I shrugged as well and went back to my ice cream.

Happy that the yelling was over, my brother and I giggled and talked about the fun adventure of that day. But we fell silent when our grandmother anxiously returned to the kitchen. She paused for a moment, leaning on the stove next to the back door looking panicked. Suddenly, the back door burst open, slamming into the stove and rattling the thin panes of its window glass. Our frantic, tear-soaked mother stood in the doorway. Without taking a step into the house, she screeched hysterically, "MY BABIES, PLEASE COME WITH ME, PLEASE!"

Frozen in bewilderment, I stared at our mother whose sobs grew stronger with each passing breath. Stunned, Grandma, reached for our jackets. "Quickly now children, come gather your boots," she coaxed, her voice strained. "But I'm not finished with my ice cream!" I shouted. "You can have ice cream at home!" our mother pleaded in a now-desperate voice.

Within a moment of slipping on our boots and jackets, our mother grabbed our wrists and dragged us down the driveway. Our grandmother stood in the doorway in shock as our grandfather consoled her. A swift chill trickled down my back. The air was freezing cold and crystallized with every exhaling breath. My feet could barely keep up as our mother pulled us faster down toward the waiting car. Her grasp tightened painfully around my wrist as she rushed us past our enraged father.

The tension was unbearable. My father's eyes locked with mine in the midst of the chaos and for a brief moment time stopped. The yelling, our movement, even my breath all seemed to freeze. I saw the tremendous pain, sorrow, anger and rage in his eyes. I knew then something was desperately wrong. I watched our father stand helplessly, arms dropped to his sides, his silhouette fading into the darkness as we drove away.

In this moment, then unknown to me, a new core belief was installed in my mind that would haunt me for many years.

Can you imagine, at just 5 years old, an experience has the power to install programs into the mind? Programs that will ultimately develop your self-worth, the decisions you will make, how you think/feel about yourself, people you will date, and the way you perceive life? Well, that's precisely what happens. Every experience, shapes, molds and develops programs that are stored in the memory banks of the subconscious mind, waiting to be launched. Throughout this book, we'll explore the impact these experiences have on our brains and how they develop into programs which, once launched, will self-validate and ultimately become your unshakeable truth.

"Can you imagine, at just age 5, an experience has the power to install programs into the mind?"

Up until about the age of five, we're primarily experiencing life emotionally. We aren't able to logically interpret the complexity of life's situations. Life is simpler and more carefree under the perceived protection of our guardians. At this stage, we have no concept of the enormity of the world, nor do we have the ability to comprehend the notion that others are having different experiences than ours. Life is taken at face value and reality appears to revolve around us.

Watching children play, it's easy to be envious of their innocence, especially when the weight of the world seems to lie on our shoulders. This naïveté is short lived however. Soon, this precious innocence is long forgotten.

Have you ever noticed that you don't have many memories prior to the age of four years old? This is

because it isn't until we reach about the age of four that we begin to develop more comprehensive cognitive thinking and start to interpret rudimentary situations. Our memory storage capacity is limited because our brains are focused on learning to comprehend complex skills.[1] Around this age the brain enters a new level of development. If you are a parent, you will recognize this as the age where "let me do it" becomes your child's mantra. It is then, and through our adolescent years, that we begin to develop an opinion about life, ourselves, society and the people in it. These "opinions" are drastically impacted by your environment and experience. Your parents, teachers, peers, TV and basically anything else you experience will shape your opinions. Your brain is like a sponge that absorbs information, draws conclusions and develops interpretations. How your brain chooses to store this information will determine the viewpoints and beliefs that will impact you for the rest of your life.

The best way to explain this is to imagine your brain as a computer. The conscious mind is the monitor, displaying images, observing and filtering information, and installing instructional code onto your hard drive. Your subconscious mind is where codes and programs are stored within the hard drive, running in the background producing images you see displayed on the desktop. Most of us are completely unaware of the programs installed on our computers,

1 Gathercole, S. (2003) The development of memory. Journal of child Psychology and Psychiatry, vol.39, No. 1, 3-27

how they work or what result they are producing. We're equally clueless about the internal functions of our minds.

Your subconscious is estimated to be controlling 80% of everything you do on a daily basis. Think about it: Do you really have to concentrate on how to brush your teeth, tie your shoes, get dressed, ride a bike or operate any other mindless function of your daily life? When you were first learning these functions, it was a different story: You had to focus all your attention and concentrate.

Think back to when you first learned to tie your shoe. You became intensely focused, tongue out to the side while singing the bunny song: "Cross the path and through the hole, up the rabbit will go..." Since tying the shoe was a new habit, we had to place our full attention on mastering it. Similarly, most beliefs in the subconscious don't get installed with just one thought. In many cases, it takes repetition and "further evidence" before a belief becomes a fully operational program functioning within the subconscious mind. Once fully operational, these programs instruct your mind on how to see, feel, and comprehend everything in your existence. These programs shape the basis of your daily interpretations. They give step-by-step instructions to your brain about how to react and interact in each situation.

"Your subconscious is estimated to be operating 80% of everything you do on a daily basis."

Similar to many of the programs operating within your computer, most programs of the subconscious are harmless and designed to simplify our processing and production time. But what happens when you get a virus or defective program installed? What havoc could result? How big an impact could these negative programs have on your decision-making, your energy levels or your overall happiness? The answer: ENORMOUS.

Experiencing the traumatic event of being physically ripped away from my father at such a young age had a devastating impact on my emotional well-being, self-development and viewpoint on life. At that pivotal moment, being just five years old, I lacked the emotional maturity to fully grasp the events taking place. All I knew was Daddy had been replaced and we were advised that he didn't love us anymore. Told to refer to him as Mr. Nobody and with little explanation, I began to think I must have done something to deserve this. At five years old, words were not up for negotiation. Words spoken were taken at face value and assumed to be the direct result of something *I* did. As every egocentric 5 year old, I had no real concept of others or the outside world. I literally, took EVERYTHING personally. Combine this with feelings of hurt, sadness and anger, and you can understand how I was left with a very powerful interpretation: "I must not be WORTHY OF LOVE."

It wouldn't be until years later that my brain would have the maturity to determine if this virus of being "unlovable" was actually true or not. However, there had been an opportunity to eliminate this belief before it became an infected virus. If my family had been aware how my young mind interpreted emotional situations, they could have helped me understand that my parents' conflict had nothing to do with me. Instead my family, like many of yours, thought they were protecting me by pretending the divorce never happened and keeping us in the dark about where our father went. Our mother (like many do) thought we were too young to remember or understand the complexity of divorce. To an extent she was right: Young children are easily distracted and don't linger on events the way adults do. It's a characteristic of younger stages of our developmental process. However, this does not mean the memory or emotion of what happened disappears. The memory stores itself in the depths of the subconscious mind waiting to be validated and ultimately launched.

As I mentioned, at its conception, a virus isn't yet a full-blown program. It still lacks the complexity and detail a real program needs to function properly. Initially, it is just a concept, a thought. It requires more support before it is completely installed. Similar to a real program that needs code, instructions, clarity and symbols to function, this belief needs proof,

evidence and other experiences to prove itself as truth. This validation process will be covered in chapters to follow. However, it's important to understand that even though this virus is not yet operational, it desperately wants to be. The mind does *not* like mystery or unanswered riddles. My subconscious mind wanted to— actually *needed* to— answer the question, "Am I lovable or not?" It will seek to solve this puzzle with every experience to follow.

If the mind revalidates and retains a belief like this, it will become a powerful core belief of the subconscious, which processes and interprets all subsequent experiences.

Now, here is where the tricky part comes in.

During this time while the brain is seeking to validate a negative belief as truth or a lie, it is naturally hardwired to NOT work in your favor. That's right: the odds are not in your favor! Ideally, it would be preferable to know you are a lovable and desirable person. However, scientific research suggests that our brains are naturally hardwired to retain, capture and recall a *negative* feeling, emotion or thought before a positive one. The odds are that this negative seed will grow into a nasty virus much faster than a positive one. This natural hardwiring is referred to as a *negative brain bias.*[2] Ironically, this serves a higher purpose.

Imagine it like this: All your memories (past and present) fill a filing cabinet. These files are not stored alphabetically, numerically, or systematically. Perceiving that negative experiences are more relevant than positive ones, your brain stores all negative memories in the front of the filing cabinet for easy

---

2 Finkenauer, Catrin; Vohs, Kathleen D. (2001). "Bad is stronger than good" (PDF). Review of General Psychology 5 (4): 323–370

13

access while tucking the positive ones toward the back. This, in its simplest context is a negative brain bias and was developed for a reason.

Throughout human evolution, it was imperative to our survival that our species learned from our mistakes and quickly identified threats. As a result, our brains learned the importance of retaining and processing negative thoughts, feelings and experiences as a means of survival. Flash-forward thousands of years. Our society has evolved into a civilized and well-protected race free of many of the threats we faced in our primitive era. Yet our brains continue to focus on negative input based on survival instincts. On top of that, the mind isn't great at differentiating between *perceived* threats and actual threats. Our modern day threats may be different, but our "fight, flight or freeze" response is as active as ever.

Why is this important? The next time you feel unworthy, not good enough, unlovable, worthless, stupid, undeserving or any other toxic belief about yourself, you can remind yourself that the feeling is part of your wiring. You aren't to blame for this. But now as an adult, you can actually *do* something about it if you are willing. The good news is, if you choose to free yourself of these toxic programs, you can work to re-wire, retrain and uninstall these old beliefs.

Detecting and removing negative core programs from your brain is similar to fixing your computer when it's infected with a virus. Initially, you may not be aware of where the problem originated or what impact it's having on your system. But if you investigate thoroughly, the root of the problem can be detected and removed, and anti-virus software can be installed. Pretending that you don't have any defective programming operating within your subconscious is like pretending computer viruses don't exist. We're all victims of defective programming. This book we will provide insights and exercises to help expose your negative core beliefs and provide tools to help overcome them.

Are you ready to permanently reboot the systematic programs that are wreaking havoc in your life?

CHAPTER 2

Identifying The Source

THE DRIVE HOME after leaving our father standing in the cold was the longest drive ever. Stone silence was only broken by the sound of the engine and our mother's sobs. Her grasp clenched tighter around my wrist with every emotional wave. Once home, our stepfather disappeared into garage, while our mother rushed us into the house and straight into our pajamas. Still perplexed by the events, neither my brother nor I felt safe asking questions, so we just quietly followed orders.

After slipping into our pajamas, our mother gathered us into her room to read us a bedtime story. I felt anxious and unsettled as we lay there listening to my mother's voice crack as she muttered the words. Looking at my brother, I could tell neither of us could follow her words. Our minds teemed with questions and our emotions were in overwhelm. Finally, my brother reluctantly asked, "We're never going to see Daddy again, are we?" Our mother froze. Staring at the book, she spit out the word "No," and continued to read.

No?! I thought. *What the heck happened?! What did we do wrong? What did she mean "no?"* Every ounce of me knew that she meant it, yet my heart yearned to know why!

I sat up, tears welling in my eyes, and asked the question that would haunt me for many years to come: "Why? Why won't we see Daddy again?" Not taking a moment to think, mother snapped, "He doesn't love us anymore. You have a new father now so you better get used to it."

Shaking and upset, she slammed the book closed and sent us to our rooms. I sat by myself in the dark trying to make sense of it all.

In the months that followed, our father called every Sunday. Our mother monitored each call, hovering over our shoulders like a hawk eyeing its prey. She forbid us from asking any questions, and prohibited us from saying "I love you" or calling him Daddy. What was supposed to be our one way to connect with our father quickly turned into a tense, uncomfortable interaction. Then one day, the calls just stopped.

Weeks turned into months, and my desperation to know the truth became unbearable.

One day, I blurted out the question I knew would get me in trouble. "Why hasn't Daddy called in a long time?" "I've told you this before," mother replied. "Mr. Nobody doesn't love us anymore. He left us. Your stepfather is your Daddy now, and you better learn to appreciate him so he doesn't leave us too." My entire little body was instantly flooded with grief and pain. I knew further questions would earn me swift punishment. I tried to hide my feelings as best I could.

At just five years of age, the traumatizing event of losing my father was quickly becoming much, much worse. A negative core belief that I was "not worthy of love" had not only been installed into my subconscious mind but also repeatedly validated by my mother's words. Without explanation or guidance, I was left to interpret this situation by myself. Like every five year old, I took this event—and everything else in my world— personally. In reality, my parents' situation had nothing to do with me. It was a battle between my mother and father, an ugly divorce between two adults. But since I was incapable of interpreting it any other way, I internalized it as my fault. "If only I would have been better, then Daddy would never have left me." And thus, one of my negative core beliefs (NCB) was born.

During the next few pages, you'll be challenged to identify your own negative core beliefs—NCBs— by exploring the pivotal life moments that shaped your current belief system and the impact they've had. By exploring carefully, we'll unearth the hidden links that lock your negative beliefs in place. With this awareness, you'll finally be able to break free of your NCBs once and for all.

Negative Core Beliefs (NCBs) are the subconscious power statements we hold to be true about ourselves and the world we live in. These beliefs are formed early in our childhood and are subsequently validated through the years by supporting "evidence" (SE). Once we adopt a power statement or negative belief as truth, we habitually look for proof to support it. We repeatedly act and react in ways that confirm this belief as "fact." This belief

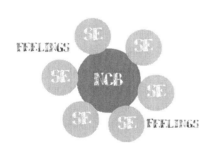

asserts itself as an "I" statement and presents itself as part of our identity. Eventually, the belief becomes so deeply ingrained, we're no longer even aware of it. Left undiscovered and unchanged, a negative belief will continue to wreak havoc in our lives as it plays out its quest to continue validating itself.

For many of you, finding your negative core belief (NCB) will be easy. It shows up as a repeating trend or repeated experience in your life. It might sound like: "No matter how hard I try, I'm just not good enough." "I can't do anything right." "Everybody I love leaves me." "I don't matter." "Life's just one struggle after another." It will sound like a reasonable statement of fact, but it's really a negative core belief proclaiming itself.

After decades of exploration and thousands of hours of coaching clients on NCB's, these ten common toxic beliefs have been discovered operating in most people:

1) **I'm unlovable** (alone, unwanted).
2) **I'm not worthy** (of love, joy, happiness, success, etc.)
3) **I don't matter** (no one cares about me, my voice or opinion doesn't matter).
4) **I am not deserving** (of joy, love, success, happiness, money, etc.).
5) **I'm not enough** (can't do anything right).

6) **I'm stupid** (not smart enough, uneducated).
7) **I have no purpose** (I'm useless, hopeless).
8) **I'm a failure** (bad, wrong, a loser).
9) **I should just die.** (It wouldn't matter if I was dead. It would be better if I was dead.)
10) **I'm weak** (not capable, can't do it).

Maybe you can immediately identify which one (or more) is present in your life. Or maybe you did not resonate with any of them. (If this is the case, revisit them after you explore your personal NCBs later in this book.) In almost all cases, toxic thoughts can be traced back to one of these ten common beliefs.

The journey of completely ridding yourself of a toxic belief virus starts back at the belief's conception. Let's use my personal story as an example. As a child, having your father torn away from you is a traumatic experience. On top of this upsetting situation, you have a close authority figure saying that "Mr. Nobody didn't love us any longer." It's pretty easy to see how I ended up with the belief that I'm not worthy of love. Of course, none of us—me as a five year old or the adults involved— realized the psychological impact the experience and conclusions I drew from it would have in shaping my viewpoint towards my life or myself.

Within every experience, we develop an interpretation based on programs that already exist in our minds. However, in most cases, if the experience happens prior to about 14 years of age, we lack personal experience for comparison. As children, we create a new interpretation for each new experience. A young, immature mind primarily develops its interpretations based on feelings and emotion rather than logic or rational thought. Since these early interpretations are based solely on emotion and since children tend to view themselves as the center of the universe, more often than not, the result is some form of personal blame or self-victimization.

In the first chapter, we discussed that a belief is first conceived through our thoughts, feelings, interpretations and experiences. In this conception stage, the belief is at its weakest and doesn't yet wreak havoc in our lives. It has little to no support or evidence, and so hasn't launched itself into an active program. If, however, these interpretations are left unchallenged and allowed to gain evidence and momentum, they will launch into a negative core belief (NCB), defective programming that can muck up your entire internal operating system.

It is probably safe to assume that you yourself are struggling with defective programing that has wreaked havoc in your life for years, if not decades. It requires much more work to detangle a NCB than an initial interpretation. Good news is, it doesn't matter if you're 15 or 50: Removing toxic programing is still possible.

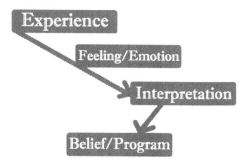

Let me break down the conception phase of a belief simply using the graphic above. Every **experience** we have will generate a **feeling and/or emotion**. From this feeling we will **interpret** the experience and form thoughts that articulate the conclusion we've drawn. This conclusion may then become our new **belief**.

For example, if as a child you **experienced (E)** <u>being wrongly punished without being allowed to defend yourself</u>, you may have **felt (F/E)** <u>worthless, unwanted, bad, angry or sad</u> and **interpreted**

(I) that <u>your side doesn't matter</u>. From this process, you very well might end up with the **Belief (B/P)** "<u>I don't matter.</u>"

At first, this new belief doesn't have much power. It is still in its infancy stage and requires nursing before it can become an uncontrollable virus. Similar to a virus getting installed on your computer, if the virus is detected and removed within the first few hours or days, it won't do much damage. However, if it's left undetected for years, your entire system will eventually break down or shut down.

The belief needs validation before it becomes entrenched as an "absolute truth." It waits lurking in the back of the subconscious mind determined to launch. It doggedly seeks to validate itself through our conscious thoughts, feelings, actions or reactions.

Again, using my personal story to demonstrate this process:

Experience: My experience was my father being absent from my life. It began as long periods of separation, and culminated in the dramatic scene at my grandparents. This was followed persistent verbal validation that "Mr. Nobody doesn't love us anymore."

Feeling/Emotion: In this experience, I felt abandoned, lonely, sad and confused.

Interpretation: Through the combination of the experience and my emotions, I drew my conclusion or interpretation. In my case it was, "I must have done something wrong for the people I love to leave me. I must not be worthy of love."

Develop Belief: A belief will be a powerful statement about yourself, life or others and typically shows up as an "I" statement. The belief I formed was "I am unworthy of love."

You may already be aware of certain negative core beliefs you operate with. But knowing your NCBs is just the start. For core transformation, you must find the source of the issue, weaken its supporting evidence (SE) and dismantle it at its core. Just like removing a virus from your computer, you must first find the source or cause of the problem. What you consciously experience (lack of self-esteem, insecurities, anxiety, fear, worry, anger, etc.) is just the symptom, *not* the cause. The cause is much deeper and more complicated than your conscious experience. The cause is locked away in your subconscious, supported by a vast amount of supporting evidence, and it requires thorough investigation to unravel the mystery.

Let's look at your potential negative core beliefs by exploring your crucial life-altering moments. The key to unlocking the cause of your subconscious beliefs is within these memories.

Homework: Identify the Source
If you already know your NCB, start here:

Write what you think your NCB is here:

_____.

(Experience) Think back to your early childhood: When do you first remember experiencing this belief?

(Feeling/Emotion) What feelings & emotions did you experience at that time? Be sure to answer from your perspective at that age, not how you feel or think you feel now as an adult.

(Interpretation) Staying with the mindset of the age you were when you experienced this traumatic event, how did you as a child (not the adult you are today) interpret that experience and those feelings?

(Belief/Program) What belief did you develop as a result of this interpretation? (This will most likely be your NCB)

If you do NOT know your NCB, start here:

(Experience) Thinking back to your childhood, what was the most traumatic or negatively impactful moment that you can remember? (Briefly write about it.)

(Feeling/Emotion) Reflecting back to that age, what feelings and emotions did you experience as a child?

(Interpretation) Staying with the mindset of the age you were when you experienced this traumatic event, how did you (not the adult you are today) interpret that experience and those feelings?

(Belief/Program) What belief do you think you developed as a result of this interpretation?

Note: Discovering your NCB is just the first step. Uncovering its source will allow us to more easily remove and permanently transform your negative belief system. This first step is the uncovering stage. Take note of what you discovered and use this insight as you continue throughout this book.

CHAPTER 3

The Validation Process

As the years passed, I began to accept that my father was truly not coming back. My young life fell into a kind of rhythm and order.

Mother fanatically embraced our stepfather's immediate family. Every holiday, birthday and special event was spent with my stepfather and his family, who welcomed us as best they could. As the years went by, I became exceedingly fond of our new family and friends.

My stepfather befriended a wealthy family who seemed to accept us like family. John, the head of this family, had built a successful business empire, and the family grew increasingly wealthy over the years. My family had always lived paycheck to paycheck eking out a living. So experiencing the wealth of John and his family was magical and exhilarating.

On one particular visit, I remember pulling into the driveway, my eight year old eyes lit up with excitement. It was a birthday celebration for John's daughter, Shelly, who was turning three. As we drove into the driveway, I imagined that I was driving into a celebrity's home. I saw the enormous playground, basketball court, and immaculate fountain. The whole family greeted us with hugs and smiles, and I felt more happy and excited than I had for months.

Within a matter of minutes, the boys were off on the skateboards. John's wife Cassie offered to show the adults through renovations taking place in the indoor gym and sauna. John picked up little Shelly and asked if I'd like to drive the golf cart. "Yes!" We got in the cart to explore the trails surrounding their 60-acre property.

John and I had a special bond. He always paid special attention to me and always protected me if the boys were being a little too rough. As we cruised along the back trails deep into the woods, he asked me about where I wanted to go in life. "I've always dreamed of going to Paris!" I blurted out. I hadn't really imagined many places in the world before, but my teacher always talked about how beautiful Paris is in the fall. It seemed like the perfect answer for someone like John. "I'm going to send you there someday, Bonnie," he promised. "I want you to see the world." *Wow!* I thought. Seeing the world never seemed like an option for me. But boy, did it sound like a grand adventure! "Oh, thank you! Thank you! I would love to see the world!" I shouted.

As we continued down the trail, John became unusually quiet. He began to stare as if something was greatly wrong. Suddenly, I felt his hand slip under my party dress. I was instantly paralyzed with fear. No one had ever touched me like this before. *Was this right?* I thought. *John wouldn't try to hurt me, would he?* As young and naïve as I was, I felt this had to be incredibly wrong.

John's face became intense as he continued to fondle me. My hands clenched tighter around the steering wheel of the golf cart as I stared at the trail in front of me. My breath froze in my chest as he pulled away. He struggled to calm his frantic breathing. After a few deep breaths, John turned to me with a smile and asked if I was alright. Unable to speak, I simply nodded.

"Let's make this our special little secret. We don't want you to get into any trouble, okay?" Still confused and petrified, I nodded in agreement.

We turned the cart around to head back to the house. John started chatting about the wonders of Paris as if nothing was different between us. And I did the only thing I knew how to do: ignore my feelings and pretend that this event had never happened.

I wish I could say that moment had been a fluke, a blip on the radar never to be repeated that I could just forget. It wasn't. That day, John opened a door he couldn't close again. As I got older and my body matured, his excitement got stronger. Our sexual encounters became more intense, and John seemed to believe that his actions were more and more acceptable.

Year after year, I kept this secret. I was afraid of getting into trouble, afraid the people I loved would leave me. I was especially afraid that this man, who gave me attention, toys, money and protection like no one else ever had, would leave me as well. But it wasn't just fear that kept me stuck. It was my NCB that I wasn't worthy of love. That NCB fed my fear, adding its emotional intensity and providing a ratio-nalization for my silence.

This new traumatic experience, though drastically different from losing my father, still became validating evidence to my original NCB. How? Well, at this point in my life, I still lacked the emotional maturity to understand the complicated dynamics in the situation with John. I wasn't equipped to look at this experience logically and objectively. It was filtered through my existing belief system, filed and stored in the memory system of an eight-year-old girl who had never been exposed to sexual predators.

This validation process locks in the power of your NCB. The memories surrounding and supporting your NCB "infect" new experiences and influences your conclusions and interpretations. But once these memories are re-wired, those same memories can ultimately set you free.

Scientists like physicist John Hagelin and Joe Dispenza now believe that the brain receives over 400 billion bits of information per second. That's right, *400 billion bits* per second. However, the brain can only register *2,000 bits* per second. [3] This means your brain *filters out over 399,999,998,000 bits of information per second*! If you think that's crazy, here's the crazi-

---

3 Joe Dispenza D.C. [2008] *Evolve Your Brain: The Science Of Changing Your Mind* Pg: 352

est part: Your mind *chooses* which pieces it wants to register.

Your brain literally selects which bits to filter out. It has to do so rapidly since every new second, another 400 billion bits of information comes its way. Whenever you walk into a room, your mind is rapidly scanning and painting a picture for you. Let's say, you walked through a room and paused to talk with someone. Your brain focuses on the conversation, but still painted a picture of the room in your mind. After leaving the room, you might recall how the room was decorated. You might remember art hanging on the wall. However you might not remember exactly what the piece looked like. It wasn't the focus of your attention so your mind chose to filter it out.

Have you ever gone into a very familiar room, and suddenly noticed a statue or piece of art on the wall you never noticed before? It didn't just arrive. Your brain probably didn't bother to register it. It was familiar, safe, and not the center of your attention. Your brain depends on commonality to help it speed through all the data. Your brain looks for patterns and familiarity to file information under the "I know what that is" folder so that it isn't wasting your valuable attention.

Remember, your attention lies in your conscious mind which only accounts for about 20% of your daily function. The mind relies on the subconscious to recognize, sort and file information quickly. That means, if the experience (E) and/or the feeling (F/E) are familiar, it files this new experience under an already existing belief (B/P) within your subconscious mind. It filters out any information it doesn't recognize, doesn't understand or doesn't assign as useful. It tends to select bits that validate *existing* belief systems.

So as you walk through life, you only *see* what you know and/or already believe. This process allows us to manage an endless stream of information, which is great. But if your existing belief system is based on a toxic virus, you've got trouble.

In my story, the belief "I am not worthy of love" had already been installed. Because this belief existed when the molestation began, my mind recognized this new experience as familiar and filed it as additional evidence that "I am not worthy." My young mind filtered through the millions of bits of information, and concluded that John was hurting me because "I wasn't worthy of being loved." In my mind with my limited information and experience, this was the *only* possible explanation. My mind rejected any other information or interpretation that did not fit my belief, thus strengthening my NCB.

You can see that there are literally trillions of possible interpretations that could come as a result of this filtration process. Your mind literally sees what it wants to see, and decides what it wants to see based on your pre-installed programming, past experiences or generational perceptions. A child under age fourteen has additional limitations. They haven't yet had much experience with life and their exposure to the complexity of the world and the people in it has been limited. They are impression-able, naive and dependent on parental figures for guidance, direction and survival (both emotionally and physically).

And sadly, children are limited by their parent's limitations as well. Many of our parent's unresolved insecurities, self-doubts, perceptions and beliefs are unconsciously handed down. This colors the emo-tionally immature interpretations we create on our own. Our society as a whole has not embraced the importance of emotional processing, healing and increasing our emotional intelligence. Most of us are not taught how to challenge our own thinking or process our feelings. We're not even taught that we have a choice in how we see, feel and interpret things. Without this knowledge, we not only limit ourselves as adults but also greatly limit the possibilities for our children.

This reminds me of an old tale someone once shared with me: One Thanksgiving dinner, three generations of families gather for a feast. One of the young great granddaughters enters the kitchen just in time to watch her mother preparing the ham to place in the oven. Her mother cuts off both ends of the ham and tosses the pieces to the side. The young girl asks why her mother did this. With a perplexed smile, her mother replies, "I'm not sure why I do that, honey. It's just always what your grandmother did. Go ask her." So the young girl finds her grandmother, plops down on her lap and asks the same question. Her grandmother giggles as she says, "That is a great question, sweetie! That's how my mother did it and her hams were always so wonderful. So I just always did it the way she did it." Determined to find out the secret, the young girl turns to her great grandmother and once again asks the question. Without any hesitation, her great grandmother announces, "I had to. Back then, my stove was too small to fit a full sized ham. I had to cut off the ends to make it fit."

The great grandmother had a reason for cutting the ham. But the next two generations mindlessly did what she did without ever questioning it. Think of this for a moment. How many things do you still do today as a result of the programs your parents installed? I'd bet that the way you fold your laundry, the brand of dish soap or toothpaste you use, even which shoe you put on first when you dress—all were programs given to you decades ago. These mindless programs might even have been passed down through several generations. This is all fine and dandy if the programs are not harmful or negative. But what about the subconscious NCB that your parents operated from? It's likely that many of those programs were unconsciously passed along and installed within the first fourteen years of your life.

In your early years, your mind gathers evidence, filters, observes, and stores information and experiences. It observes how to be a mother, father, wife, husband, daughter or brother. We observe and learn how to handle money, make fashion choices and even process emotions. If your parent was obsessed with dieting or cleaned when she was angry, you observed this as a child then adopted or rejected the pattern. It's like the old saying. "Monkey see, monkey do."

Many of my clients are obsessed with how clean their house is, how much they eat, or how successful they are as a direct result of an unconscious NCB that their parents acted out and never questioned. Around the age of fourteen dormant programs have collected enough evidence to come to life and begin influencing our behaviors.

Whether the NCB was installed directly from personal experience or handed down generationally, this virus is affecting—or *infecting*— how you perceive new situations. If you believe you're not good enough, think of how many opportunities you have during a week to "prove" this as true. Endless.

The brain interprets experiences along with the feelings associated with them then categorizes them in our memory banks as either a new belief or validation of one we already have. If the belief we already have installed is negative, any new experiences act as reinforcement locking the old belief in place. With each new validation, your NCB gains power. Year after year, it grows stronger in the dark corners of the mind until it reaches critical mass to become true to your core.

The pivotal moments such as losing my father and being molested installed my NCB, but it required further support to launch into a fully functional program. As years passed and my mind developed, new questions of "What if?" and "Why?" began to nag at me.

So in my experience, the break down was:

BELIEF: I am not worthy.

SUPPORTING EVIDENCE: From earliest memory to 14 years old:

EXPERIENCE: Father no longer loves you. (BELIEF VALIDATED)

EXPERIENCE: Being sexually molested. (BELIEF VALIDATED)

EXPERIENCE: Being rejected by friends in school. (BELIEF VALIDATED)

EXPERIENCE: Kicked out of band because I wasn't good. (BELIEF VALIDATED)

EXPERIENCE: Being beat up and bullied. (BELIEF VALIDATED)

EXPERIENCE: Having the boy I like ditch me. (BELIEF VALIDATED)

Multiply this list by hundreds of other little examples and I ended up with one powerful belief. Now as an adult looking back at each event, I can understand the complexity and uniqueness within each one. Yet before age fourteen, my mind couldn't fully grasp their complexity. So it filtered them through my existing negative belief system. I internalized each experience as happening because I wasn't good enough, therefore not worthy. Not worthy of love, support, understanding, friendship, living—virtually everything!

With each additional validation, the self-loathing, self-hatred, and attitude of worthlessness became more intense. Left unchallenged, my program was ready to launch with full force and was bound to have drastic implications on my life to come.

Typically the more painful or traumatic the experience you have, the *stronger* the core belief will become. In my situation, it wasn't until after being molested that my core belief became locked in. Having someone take advantage of you sexually at just eight years old is a pretty traumatic experience. Conflicting emotions of fear, panic, trust and confusion all flood your emotional body within an instant. You don't know whether to scream, yell, fight, run or hide and your emotional system goes into fight, flight or freeze.

As the sexual abuse continued, I started emotionally and mentally checking out. This numbness became frequent. Becoming numb, completely detached from the situation and my emotions somehow made it all okay. The fear of losing everyone I loved kept me confined in this mental trap. As a tween (preteen), we all develop a better understanding of self and become better at expressing our feelings. However for me, it felt unsafe to do so. So my immature viewpoint and perceptions were left unchallenged, thus validating my NCB.

According to *The Abel and Harlow Child Molestation Prevention Study*, Over 39 *million* adults have been sexually molested.[4] Of the 39 million adults who survived child sexual abuse, 68% were sexually abused by a member of their own family and 40% were molested by someone within their social circle. Another study states that one out of every four girls and one out of every six boys are sexually abused prior to the age of eighteen.[5] That means that many people reading this

---

4 http://www.childmolestationprevention.org/pages/study.html

5 National Child Traumatic Stress Network [2009] *Child Sexual Abuse Fact Sheet* PDF

book have a similar story to my own. If you are one of them, know that you can truly transform this terrible experience and finally shift it to inner peace.

Deep within my subconscious mind, the belief that I was not worthy (of love, acceptance, respect, joy, success, etc.) was festering, gaining momentum and looking for opportunities to validate itself. I would never claim that, at eight years old, I attracted this predator into my life. But because the belief of not being worthy was already lurking in my mind, this situation validated it perfectly and helped shape my viewpoint of the world and the people within it. My mind filtered and filed this data as proof that my existing negative belief was true. Combine this negative belief with strong emotions, and my NCB got locked in tighter than a maximum-security prison with no visible escape.

Feelings are the guards that stand watch over the belief, ensuring it will not escape.

Flash forward to about age fourteen: This is where the trouble really begins. My negative belief has enough evidence to become *true to my core.* It is locked in with a tremendous amount of pain, hurt, shame, guilt, fear and anger—the perfect concoction for a path of self-destruction. Right around fourteen, we start developing strong emotional beliefs and opin-ions. We start reacting more to life and the unresolved emotions brewing under the surface. Our chemical bodies are flooded with hormones, and we realize how much power or control we have. At this stage, we can't pinpoint the cause of all our feelings or emo-tions and how or why they are impacting us. All we knew is the echoing voice within our heads repeating, "You're just not good enough" and "No one loves you" or "You're stupid, just give up now." It's like leaving the doors open and unguarded at the maximum-secu-rity prison, hoping the inmates won't try to escape. Ha! Good luck with that.

In our tween years, we start to develop a deeper sense of self-identity. School, socially and physical transformations add immense amounts of pressure along with confusion and anxiety. We compare our-selves harshly to others and make rash judgments. We're still generally rather optimistic. But the closer we get to the teen years, the more our internal belief systems start to run the show.

During this transition, we are most vulnerable and susceptible. We're emotionally raw and exposed, unable to articulate or process complex emotions and situations. If trauma, dysfunction or abuse in any shape or form is present, it's even worse. For many of us, childhood felt more like an episode of *Survivor* than *Leave it to Beaver*. Our most painful memories come from childhood, and it still impacts the decisions we make today.

Think back to entering high-school. This is most likely when the inner rebel started to emerge, or the perfectionist, the I-don't-care attitude, the partier, the master procrastinator or a myriad of other external expressions of self.

Your fight, flight and freeze response was in full bloom. If you chose fight, some of things you experienced might have been: failing school or sports, rebelling at school or with teachers, experimenting with drugs, getting in trouble with the law, partying or ignoring authority.

If you chose flight, you probably threw yourself into school or sports, became a straight-A student, teacher's pet or "yes" man, feared getting into trouble, had thoughts of suicide, didn't hang out with peers, stayed home or in your room, rarely spoke up unless spoken to, dressed in dark clothes, or became withdrawn, depressed or lonely.

If you chose to freeze, you might have been absent-minded, disinterested in anything, emotionally detached, withdrawn, paralyzed by questions or signs of trouble, prone to panic attacks, and caught in obsessive worry or fear.

In my particular case, at fourteen I started to rebel and sought acceptance anywhere I could get it. The overwhelming feeling of not being worthy grew bigger, stronger and more painful by the day. Internally I was plagued with feelings of hurt, shame, anger and hopelessness. At this age I was still being molested, abused, ignored, rejected and punished. Feeling alone and unable to escape the negative emotions, I sought ways to numb the pain. I became isolated from my family, not feeling accepted or understood, and emotionally haunted by the secret of my sexual abuse and unanswered questions of my absent father. Guilt and shame consumed my mind: "I should know better. I was old enough to do something about it. This must be my fault!" So I did what any rational child would do who was seeking approval: I took it from the first people I perceived as accepting me—the misfits, trouble makers and drug addicts. And so began a seemingly endless cycle of one negative validation after another.

During this vulnerable age, your subconscious negative core beliefs are kicked into overdrive. Once-dormant NCB are now fully operational programs, feeding your conscious thoughts, feelings, and actions while shaping the perceptions of your experiences. All of your conscious thoughts, feelings, actions and reactions are aligned with your NCB which perpetuates the problem. With each validation, this belief becomes so entrenched into who you are that it becomes *true to your core*.

Throughout this chapter, we have explored how a negative core belief (NCB) gets validated, gains momentum and ultimately launches as a fully operational program using my story. Now it's your turn. In the last chapter, you identified the source of your NCB. In this next section, you'll unmask the supporting evidence that keeps your NCB locked into place.

Remember that, without evidence, this NCB has no weight. Imagine that you're in court with a defense attorney, prosecuting attorney, and judge. The prosecuting attorney has been gathering evidence over the years to prove to the judge why your NCB is true. Up until now, the defense attorney hasn't shown up to prove otherwise. So the judge had no choice but to rule in the favor of the prosecutor. To fully transform your NCB, you must act like a defense attorney and poke holes in the evidence. You must create enough reasonable doubt so the judge cannot convict.

Without knowing what evidence the prosecutor has against us, we wouldn't have a chance of winning in court. So, let's expose your evidence!

Homework: Exposing your validating evidence.

Step 1: Explore

Think back into your history. Remember all the times you felt your Negative Core Belief (NCB). Example: If your NCB is "I'm not good enough," when was a particular time you felt that way?

The objective is to uncover as much evidence as you can. The more evidence you uncover, the easier it will be to uninstall this toxic program. If you struggle, try going back in time in 5-10 year increments. Think about where you were during that time of your life, who you hung around, where you worked, what trips you took, or who you were dating.

Step 2: Journaling exercise

Reflecting on your supporting evidence, write a mini version of what happened for each incident. Then ask yourself:

- In what ways does this story support my NCB?
- How are the two connected?
- What thoughts or fears do I have surrounding this experience?
- What fears (if any) do I have about letting this validating evidence go?
- What kind of impact did this experience have on my life?
- In what ways is this evidence still affecting my life today?
- In what ways would my life be different if I was to let this go?
- What is something positive I have learned about myself or life because of this experience?

CHAPTER 4

Thought Tornado of Destruction

As THE YEARS went by, I found myself seeking acceptance from anyone I could get it from. In my sophomore year of high school, I must have changed my look, how I talked and who I hung out with at least a dozen times. I was a chameleon, adapting to my surroundings for survival, trying to stay under the radar yet still noticeable enough to be worthy. Unaware that my NCB was fully functional, fueling my conscious thoughts, feelings and actions, I found myself grasping for acceptance from anyone willing to give it to me. I had a lonely, achy feeling inside. Despite my desperate attempts to fit in, I never truly felt like I belonged. I jumped from relationship to relationship, transforming my interests, hobbies, likes and dislikes in a desperate attempt to be loved.

The stronger the feeling that I didn't belong became, the more daring I became to fit in. I started taking extreme risks with my life. The crazier I became, the more attention I seemed to get. The pain wallowing up inside was so thick, some days I felt like I couldn't breathe. I found friends who understood my pain and struggled to deal with their own. Drugs, drinking, skipping school, breaking the law and lies were all part of a normal day. Yet underneath it all, I yearned to be good, so I maintained at school and work just enough just enough just enough to pass and not get fired.

It wasn't until the ultimate betrayal by my boyfriend and family that I spiraled completely out of control.

In a rare moment of trust, I shared my darkest secret to my boyfriend of one year, swearing him to secrecy. I felt sweet relief as he comforted me, swearing he wouldn't tell a sole. Knowing that promises are often broken, I should have known this was a secret he couldn't keep. Within weeks, counselors, child protective services and police officers all invaded my life and turned my family's world upside down.

My parents dismissed my brothers to their rooms to protect them from hearing such vile claims against their favorite family friend. As I shared my story, my parents shook their heads in disbelief, doing their best to understand the situation.

Fearing repercussions of telling this horrible secret, I disappeared for weeks at a time. This wasn't that uncommon as I often went on bingers and stayed with friends. The dust seemed to settle and no doomsday was brought down around my head. I began to feel confident that it all might just disappear. Then one day I was asked to come home.

As soon as I entered the driveway, my parents put me in the car to go to a meeting with them. I panicked. "We're not going to see him, are we?" I pleaded. They said that we weren't but gave no further information. The 30-minute car ride was filled with tense silence.

We ended up at an attorney's office. Cassie, John's wife, met us in the waiting room and embraced me with a grizzly bear hug. "I'm so sorry" she whispered. Tears streamed down her face.

The four of us were ushered into an office. An older man sat across the table. "John has admitted his wrongs and we want you to know we are sorry this has happened to you," he said. "With that in mind, your family wants to do everything they can to keep the family together and not send John to jail. The only way we can do that is if you are willing not to press charges. If you choose to press charges, you'll break up their family and send John to jail. This would cause a lot of hardship and require a public conviction. Now, you don't want all that trouble do you?"

Everyone turned to me. I felt an overwhelming shame wash over me like a tsunami as my family shared more details of this plan. If I agreed to sign, swearing I made this whole thing up, they promised John would be sent to treatment and I would get the help I needed. All expenses would be covered. I felt trapped, betrayed, vulnerable. I agreed to the terms, signed the paperwork and was silent the whole ride home.

Unfortunately for me, the plan failed. Sexual interactions with John continued. Once again, I was left with a dark secret. Only now, I was convinced there was nowhere to turn. Everything, except me, went back to normal. Every holiday and birthday once again spent as "a family" and the "incident" was swept under the rug, never to be talked about again. Plunging into the deep end of darkness, I turned to the streets in a desperate need of escape. I abandoned any rights to my own well-being. I allowed John and any other man I dated to have their way with me.

My negative core belief was out of control and all of my conscious thoughts, feelings and actions expressed my absolute worthlessness.

When your subconscious programs have gathered the support they need to launch, they grab hold of your behaviors and can influence your conscious thinking. In this story, my belief system was fully operational and I was perfectly capable of making my own decisions. However, I was still predominantly making emotional decisions directed by my pre-installed belief programming.

My subconscious belief of "not being worthy" had gathered enough evidence to declare itself as truth. It was locked deep into my mind, hidden from even my own consciousness. If anyone would have walked up to me and said, "You really look like you are struggling with feeling worthy," I probably would have laughed them off— or punched them in the face—without stopping to consider if there was any truth in the statement.

The subconscious mind does not always make it easy to identify programming. In fact, there is a protective shield that surrounds many of your strong negative belief systems. That defensive shield is called *denial*. Your mind is so powerful it has the ability to block out, hide and suppress painful thoughts, feelings and memories. It doesn't delete them, just creates barriers around them as a means of self-protection. This self-protective mode is strongest when you feel weak or vulnerable. Denial is a major theme of our tween and teenage years. At this stage, you are too close to your childhood to be aware of its impact on your emotional and mental well-being. The tendency to be egocentric—it's all about me— still exists and you're unable to be objective about what happened to you. Your mind is still set on taking things personally, yet as a teen, you're armed with the illusion of control and know-it-all attitude.

The teenager's programming is fully functional. However, they are still mostly incapable of understanding and dealing with the tremendous complexities of the mind. Unless you are made aware of the impact your subconscious beliefs have on your conscious thoughts, feelings and actions or reactions, you stay victim to repeating the same hardship and drama over and over again.

You've probably read about the principle of changing your life by changing your thinking in all sorts of self-help books. Planting a new "truth" in your conscious thinking is valid. However it isn't the sole answer. If you do not change your *subconscious* beliefs as well, then all the time and effort you place into changing just your conscious thoughts will fall short.

In *The Biology of Belief*, Dr. Bruce Lipton wrote:

"When it comes to sheer neurological processing abilities, the subconscious mind is millions of times more powerful than the conscious mind. If the desires of the conscious mind conflict with the programs in the subconscious mind, which 'mind' do you think will win out? You can repeat the positive affirmation that you are loveable over and over or that your cancer tumor

will shrink. But if, as a child you heard over and over again that you are worthless and sickly, those messages programmed in your subconscious mind will undermine your best conscious efforts to change your life."

The conscious and subconscious aspects of the mind are operating simultaneously at any given time. The conscious mind is the one we understand and control. It remembers to take out the trash and pick up the kids. The subconscious mind works alongside the conscious mind and directs your habits. The subconscious mind is the core basic operating system on your hard drive. It's where we store our fundamental belief systems, habits and behaviors.

As I mentioned earlier, your subconscious mind is estimated to control 80% of everything you do on a daily basis. Everything from how you brush your teeth to how you handle getting cut off in traffic are preprogrammed within your subconscious mind. Whether they were installed through our own perception system or learned from someone else, these programs directly impact our conscious thoughts feelings, actions and reactions.

The conscious and the subconscious mind affect and influence one another. Subconscious programs are initiated by interpretations of experiences, feelings and emotions. They require support or repetition before they lock into the unconscious mind as truth. Once they lock however, they become your default programs. With these programs in place, we function on auto-pilot, mindlessly acting and reacting to life versus choosing our response. The longer you live unaware of this dynamic and the longer you avoid taking personal responsibility for changing it, the longer you will suffer needlessly.

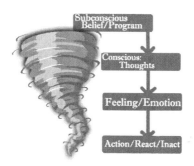

In my story, the thought of being worthless entered my mind at age five and gathered evidence until I was age fourteen. Then, left unchallenged, it launched as my default programming which then influenced my conscious "choices." Defaulting to installed programs is unconscious. My choosing and thinking was on autopilot, which restricted me from even seeing other possibilities or choices.

As a juvenile, I was ignorant and completely unaware (like most of us are) of the role I played in my own suffering. Though the abuse was horrible and not in my control, my suffering could have been lessened with the proper insight. Unfortunately, we're all limited by our family's limitations as well. My family wasn't equipped to handle the situation. So they did the only thing their own subconscious belief systems knew how to do: fight, flight or freeze. My family's fight/flight/freeze response was as intense as mine. They were just as oblivious as I was when it came to understanding conscious versus subconscious beliefs, which caused them to react as they did.

Once your NCB accepts itself as truth, it fuels all your conscious thoughts, feelings, actions and reactions, spinning them into a tornado of destruction. Every person you date, hang out with, or interact with has to fit within your belief system. Your mind filters through all the information available and only selects the 2,000 pieces that are familiar.

"Once Your Programing accepts itself as truth, it fuels all your conscious thoughts, feelings, actions, and reactions, spinning them into a tornado of destruction."

For example, your negative core belief is: I don't matter. You date someone who is frequently late but who is otherwise very attentive and affectionate. Your conscious thoughts begin to obsess over the fact that they are always late. Based on your NCB, you conclude that they don't care about you enough to be on time, completely dismissing how affectionate and attentive they are. You begin to *feel* that they don't care, and react angrily every time they're late. You push them away (action). As a result, the belief of "I don't matter" is validated. The other information of affection and attentiveness was in front of you. Yet the mind focused on what your default program instructed it to do. If the belief didn't exist, your thoughts, feelings and reaction in that situation would be different.

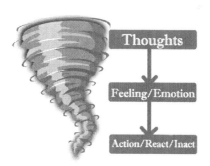

The subconscious mind gives step-by-step instructions to the conscious mind, telling it what to see, feel, hear and perceive. The more defective programing, the more pain, suffering and heartache you experience.

Once my programing launched, I only noticed times I did something that wasn't good enough, when I wasn't accepted or felt unworthy. My conscious mind couldn't see anything else. This was my reality. I believed to my core that I wasn't worthy. All experiences including the sexual abuse, were filed and filtered through this belief, validating themselves over and over again.

Here's what it looked like:

Subconscious *Program/Belief*: I am not worthy

Conscious *thoughts* - spinning as a result of the subconscious program:

- My boyfriend told my secret because he didn't truly love me.
- My family believes this is my fault.
- No one loves me enough to protect me.
- I'm not worthy of protection.
- Not even my father wants me.
- Why should I try? No one thinks I will ever amount to anything anyways.
- I am so worthless.

Conscious *feelings* - fueled by my conscious thought:

- Depression
- Worthlessness
- Hopelessness
- Self-pity
- Shame
- Guilt

Conscious *Action/Reaction/Inaction* - driven by feelings:

- Obsessive drinking & drug use to escape from feelings
- Panic attacks
- Suicide attempts
- Cutting
- Rebelling against authority

My actions, reactions and inactions (A/R/I) were directly correlated to the overwhelming feelings I was desperately trying to avoid. My feelings (F) fueled my thinking (T) and my thinking (T) was directly influenced by my subconscious NCB. The perfect storm.

Your thoughts (T) become your feelings (F) which ultimately drive your actions, reactions or inactions (A/R/I). If you are wondering what an inaction is, a good example would be procrastination, avoidance, or shutting down.

> *"Your beliefs become your thoughts, your thoughts become your words,*
> *your words become your actions, your actions become your habits,*
> *your habits become your values, your values become your destiny."*

—MAHATMA GANDHI

Your conscious mind has a cause-and-effect process and boils down to this simple process: Your NCB influences your Thoughts (T) which generate Feelings (F) which fuels your Actions/Reactions/Inaction (A/R/I).

No conscious feeling exists without a thought and no action or reaction exists without a feeling or avoidance of a feeling fueling it. Thoughts can exist *outside* the NCB and can generate different feelings and actions.

And since most information passes through your feeling center of your brain prior to the cognitive part, feelings can initiate without thoughts. That said, many of the default actions and reactions you currently experience are a direct result of your subconscious programming. Your brain's filtrations system is skewing your perception. So to transform your life, it's essential to transform subconscious beliefs along with conscious beliefs.

You need to transform both the conscious and subconscious levels if you want to end the repetitious cycle of negative behaviors, feelings and thoughts. Here is the cool news: Your consciousness thoughts (T), feelings (F), and actions/reactions/inaction (A/R/I) and your subconscious NCB *can* be changed. Both require work, and neither will transform overnight. You'll have to put forth the effort, engage in deep reflection, develop consistency and use your willpower. And it will take some time.

I love this quote by Stephen Covey: *"Every human has four endowments - self-awareness, conscience, independent will and creative imagination. These give us the ultimate human freedom… The power to choose, to respond, to change."* These four endowments are truly some of mankind's greatest freedoms. Too many of us, however, don't appreciate or use them. We operate day-to-day unaware of what we think, how we feel and why we react in certain ways. We don't allow our conscience to guide us, or use our independent will to change what we know needs changing.

In his book[6] published in 1910, Wallace Wattles wrote:

> *"Every man has the natural and inherent power to think what he wants to think, but it requires far more effort to do so than it does to think the thoughts which are suggested by appearances. To think according to appearances is easy; to think truth regardless is laborious, and requires the expenditure of more power than any other working man is called upon to perform."*

It's true: Change requires work! The question is, how ready and willing are you to make this change reality?

No one in this world has the power to transform you from the inside out. Let me repeat that: ___NO ONE can do this work for you___. Others can guide you and provide you with the tools necessary to transform. But no one outside of you can change you without your permission. You have to choose this journey and put your feet on the path. You'll face challenges. But if you choose to face them head on, you can transform

---

6 *The Science of Getting Rich* by Wallace Wattles

your life! This book provides you with tools, insight and exercises to help you reclaim your authentic self. If you find yourself getting stuck or needing further guidance as you progress, I am here to support you along this journey at www.BonnieKelly.me.

Homework: TFA Tracker

We don't all follow the same roadmap. We're all unique individuals who have experienced completely different variables throughout our lives that lead us to our results. Like that old saying, no two snowflakes are exactly alike. No two people develop exactly alike. In fact, it's neurologically impossible for two people to process and think identically. But certain influences can help explain and alter your actions and reactions to situations. Your actions and reactions in your life are a direct result of your thoughts and feelings.

As Gandhi said, "*Your beliefs become your thoughts, your thoughts become your words, your words become your actions, your actions become your habits, your habits become your values, your values become your destiny.*"

This teaching has ancient roots. Modern quantum physics and neuroscience has revealed how important this truly is. Your subconscious programs directly influence your conscious thoughts and your conscious thoughts create your feelings, which ultimately form your actions (or reactions). Scientists can measure these conscious thoughts in the brain. With mindfulness, we can trace them ourselves.

If you've completed the exercises from previous chapters, you've already spent considerable time uncovering and examining your NCB and its supporting evidence. Now let's focus on the conscious aspects and discover the patterns and habits your NCB is influencing.

During the next few weeks, monitor and track your conscious thoughts, feelings, behaviors, actions and reactions to life. Practicing self-awareness and consciously focusing on your (T) (F) and (A/R/I) puts you back into the driver's seat and allows you to make the changes you want in the present moment. Throughout the next few weeks, use a pocket-size notebook to write down all your thoughts (T) feelings (F) and actions/reactions/inactions (A/R/I) that are negative or out of alignment with your highest desires. This notebook will become your TFA Tracker. Keep your notebook on you or within arm's reach so you can capture the T, F, A/R/I in any moment. It's been estimated that you have over 60,000 thoughts traveling through your mind on any given day, so it will be impossible to capture *all* of your thoughts. Don't worry if you miss a few, thousand. What you want is to identify patterns and negative habits you haven't noticed previously.

Thoughts (T): Simply jot down any negative thought, judgment, blame, or criticism towards yourself or others. Your objective is to become intimately aware of your thoughts because they lead to your actions/reactions/inactions. If you're not used to monitoring your thoughts, this might be a challenge until you form a habit. Once you have written down the negative (T), counter it with something positive. You don't necessarily need to believe the counter. At this stage, we are just practicing a new habit. You can counter it with a positive affirmation or disproving statement (statement that disputes the original negative thought). Then see if you can identify the NCB that directly relates to this negative thought or judgment, and counter that NCB with a positive affirmation.

Feelings (F): If you have trouble capturing your thoughts, try starting with feelings. Pay attention any time you find yourself feeling hurt, upset, angry, anxious, worried, stress, ashamed, inadequate, fearful, depressed, lonely, unappreciated, worthless, hopeless, etc. Pause for a moment. Take a deep, slow breath and then note the feeling in your TFA Tracker. Once you've noted the feeling, try to identify the Thought (T) that stimulated the feeling, as well as the NCB Linked to it. Next, counter the feeling, thought and NCB with positive affirmations or disproving statements.

Actions/Reactions/Inactions (A/R/I): In many cases, you might find yourself in actions or reactions before you even noticed thoughts or feelings. In this case, don't beat yourself up! Simply note down the Action: unmotivated, avoidance, defensiveness, depressed, isolation, low energy, lashing out, procrastinating, not doing what you say you will, lying etc. Once you identify the action/reaction (or inaction), do a self-check-in. Can you identify the feeling? If so, trace it back to the thought, then back to the NCB. Repeat the affirmation process.

After a few weeks of tracking your thoughts, feel-ings, and action/reactions, ask yourself:

- What patterns have I discovered?
- How are these patterns connected to my NCB?
- What can I start doing right now to help me change my T, F, A/R/I?

CHAPTER 5

A Shift in Perspective

THE 16-HOUR DRIVE to Mississippi was a long one. I made the decision to move quickly, once again feeling the need to run. The drugs no longer worked. No amount or combination could numb the pain and hate that raged in my heart. A few weeks before, I'd been raped, fired and publicly humiliated. I'd had enough. So I packed up everything I owned in my car and headed to Mississippi with my best friend and her boyfriend looking for a positive change.

The five years leading up to my 19th birthday had been difficult. I had caused myself and those around me a tremendous amount of pain by being strung out on drugs, drinking and what many would call prostitution. I felt ashamed and disgusted at who I had become. I hated myself, I hated my life and more than anything I prayed God would take me from this wretched place. *"God, I know you may have forgotten about me by now, but if there ever was a time to give me a break, now would be it."*

I was alone in the car for the final stretch into Biloxi. My friend jumped into her boyfriend's car a few miles back. I followed behind them, mesmerized by the brilliant lights of the shoreline casinos. It took me a few moments to notice the cop lights in my rearview mirror. Normally, I'd be in full panic in this situation, frantically making up a story to get me out of trouble. But I'd been clean for the past few days and had no drugs on me. I felt comfortable letting the officer search the car. What I didn't realize is that my friend had left her purse with all her goodies on the passenger floorboard. Within an hour, I found myself in jail, then on probation with heavy fines. *"Why is this shit always happening to me?!"* I thought over and over.

Crushed by yet another failed start, I went on another binge, this time with a guy who was deeply troubled and had no regard for his life or mine. Heading to Mississippi was supposed to be my escape from the turmoil and pain. Instead, I found myself in an even bigger mess than the one I'd left. *"What have I done to deserve this?! How do I always get myself in situations like these?!"* After about a year in Mississippi, I fled once again.

I jumped from state to state like a gypsy, hoping with each fresh start would magically give me a new life. From Mississippi to Alabama to Ohio and back to Michigan. Each stay was shorter than the last. Despite my best intentions, trouble seemed to follow me everywhere. It never occurred to me that I might be the cause of my own trouble. Each situation, piercingly painful with its own brand of drama, seemed unique and separate. Yet all the situations were oddly similar. My thoughts centered on mantras like *"It's just one bad thing after another"* and *"Nothing ever goes right for me."* Completely unaware of the impact my mindset played in my life, I continued to be disempowered by each new turn of events.

What I definitely needed at this stage of my life was a shift in perspective. Perspective is what shapes your reality. It is the way you choose to see the world around you and the people in it, how you participate and fit into this world. Your perceptions are based on your past experiences and your underlying beliefs. They affect how you experience all new situations, your decision-making and how you choose to act, treat or manage those around you.

"Your perceptions are based on your past experiences and your underlying beliefs, and they affect how you experience all new situations."

Imagine wearing rose-colored glasses your whole life. The sky would always appear to have a reddish tone to it. You'd grow up thinking and believing this was the true color of the sky. Most likely, you wouldn't even question it. Though the rest of the world would see the sky as blue, you'd have a completely different experience because of your perspective. Now imagine taking the glasses off for the first time. The experience would be unsettling and mind-blowing. This different experience would challenge all you believed to be the truth up until this point.

Your belief system and NCB operates like those rose-colored glasses altering your reality. At this point in my personal story, I experienced life through the lenses of worthlessness. Everything I saw, felt, heard and experienced passed through these "I'm worthless"-  colored glasses altering my reality. For true transformation, we have to remove our glasses, challenge the old perceptions that were based on our old belief operating system and choose to change the way we look at the past. In other words, shift our perspective.

On a neurological level, your brain is unique to you. In fact it is so unique, you can consider yourself an endangered species! How you think, act, react, interact, interpret, perceive and experience life all depends on how your brain neurologically wired itself. The combination of possibilities are endless! No one has ever walked in your shoes, lived what you have lived, felt exactly what you have felt in the same manner that you have. Yet, we compare, judge, ridicule and persecute ourselves and others for "not understanding" or "not knowing better." Yet, how could we?

Your brain makes associations and "wires" itself based on experience and perception. You may feel that love equals pain or that wants equal disappointment or that promises equal lies. However you're hardwired, your belief is linked to a past experience, emotion and memory. To transform your NCB at the source, we have to shift the perception that encircles this belief and all the supporting evidence that keeps it in power.

The first step in this process is realizing you have a choice. That's right, a choice. A choice in how you look at, think about, react to and feel about each situation, past and present. You don't have a choice in what happened. The past is the past. Your history has been written and can't be changed. But what can be changed, is how you choose to think about and hold onto that past.

I love this quote by Omar Khayyam and it is one I have heard the late Wayne Dyer use often. Omar wrote, *"The Moving Finger writes; and, having writ, moves on: nor all thy piety nor wit shall lure it back to cancel half a line, nor all thy tears wash out a word of it."* He is saying that it doesn't matter how much you cry, scream, hate, fight, worry or resent it, nothing will change what has been written. We waste so much of our precious lives in the regrets or sorrows of our history when there is *nothing* you can do to change what has been done. Life moves on. The question is, will you? To move on, we must recognize how our perceptions of the past are vastly limiting our happiness of today.

"We waste so much of your precious lives in the regrets or sorrows of our history when there is nothing you can do to change what has been done."

While sitting in a restaurant with eighty other people, has it ever occurred to you that each person is having their own unique experience? One person is glowing with joy over the food and service, one is bitterly unhappy, one is ungrateful while another is deeply grateful. They all are in the same restaurant, getting similar service and eating the same level of food. Yet each diner is choosing his or her own unique experience. Based on their memories or experiences from the past, they will focus on one or two elements of the experience and remain oblivious to the rest. Even if the food or service is horrible, it is your choice to have a bad experience or not. Your experience does not *have* to suck in *any* situation— unless you choose for it to suck.

When a sucky dining experience happens to me (and from time to time it does), I choose to laugh at the experience. I try to shift the waitress's mood by talking to her and being kind. I expand my perception, recognize the waitress is having her own unique experience. I choose to not take the experience personally. I know it is my choice to focus on having a bad time or not. I also know I can influence others around me. I often remind myself: "I have a happiness disease and it's my job to infect as many people as I can!" Same goes for smiling and kindness. I loved the ad by Liberty Mutual Insurance: Someone observes another person doing something kind. Later that day, the observer does something kind for someone else, and the chain of kindnesses continues. It's easy to spread kindness and generosity as it is to spread anger and hate. Our emotions influence and affect those around us, and each one of us possesses the power to use them for good or evil.

"Emotions influence and affect those around us and each one of us possesses the power to use them for good or evil."

Knowing you have a choice is a power unmatched by any other, and you can totally transform your life by embracing this knowledge

As I moved from state to state I brought my troubles and sorrows with me. It didn't matter how far I ran from them, 100 miles or 2,500 miles. Wherever I was, they were too. It wasn't until much later that I understood that *I* was the main character in my story of suffering. It was only then that I could begin my healing process. And it was through the discovery of choice and understanding perspective that I realized I could completely alter how I felt, the experiences I had, the people I met. I could now transform the impact my past had on me.

To shift your perception, you need to understand that each emotion we experience has an impact on our mental, emotional and physical well-being. Emotions either have a constructive, destructive or neutral impact on us. The longer the emotion is left unprocessed and/ or harbored in the body, the more destructive impact it can have on our overall well-being. Understanding the impact emotions have on you, how they affect your decisions and why you choose to react the way you do, will help you increase your emotional intelligence dramatically.

Emotional Intelligence (EI) is having the capacity to be aware of, control, and express your emotions, and to handle interpersonal relationships judiciously and empathetically. Increasing your EI is one of the most powerful skills you can develop.

The easiest way to determine whether an emotion is constructive or destructive is to check into how it feels and how you respond when experiencing it. When you're feeling ashamed, guilty, sad, hurt, rejected, hopeless, or depressed, how do you feel? No energy, low, wanting to hide, never leaving the bed, disconnected, withdrawn? What about anger, blame, judgment, criticism? How do those make you feel? More energetic but tense, on edge, wanting to explode, lashing out, violent? Both examples are destructive emotions. They are natural responses to certain situations and healthy to experience. But when they remain in your body for long periods of time, when you cannot let go of the hurt, anger or pain (either directed towards yourself or another), then these emotions can have devastating impacts on your overall physical, mental and emotional well-being.

Some of the greatest pains we harbor steam from our childhoods. As a former childhood survivor, I understand completely how you feel, but I'm guessing you're not reading this book for empathy. You are reading it to transform your NCB and get your life on track. So, here's your wake-up call: If you do not shift your perceptions into healing, forgiveness, love, empathy and compassion for yourself and those who have harmed you, you will continue to *validate* the negative beliefs those memories are protecting.

The longer you hold on and withhold forgiveness, empathy, or understanding, the stronger your NCB will remain. As we discussed earlier, your NCB requires evidence and the emotional pain surrounding it to stay fully functional. Take away the evidence, you take away the power. Can you guess who is 100% responsible for accomplishing this? You are.

How? Remember when we talked about how the brain filters our experiences through our already existing belief systems before it labels it? These labels are all assumptions based on our perceptions. Our perceptions are those NCB-colored glasses that distort what we see, and how we feel about and internalize an experience. We interpret the experience and make an assumption about it.

For example, let's say the negative core belief you operate from is "Nothing I do is ever enough" (which easily translates into "I'm not enough"). At work, where you always feel underappreciated and criticized, one day you walk past the water cooler and see two female colleagues whispering to one another. As you approach, they stop talking, and awkwardly change the conversation. Now, filter this experience as someone who feels they are not enough and what do you think your assumptions would be?

Those assumptions might sound something like: "They were talking about me, I know they don't like me, I don't like them anyway. I should get another job where people appreciate me." The mind automatically assumed the worst. Left unchallenged, it will file this experience as further evidence under the belief that "I'm not good enough." But let's analyze this for a moment. Do we know for sure they were talking about you? Even if your gut reaction is "yes," the reality is no. Unless you directly heard what they were talking about or were participating in the conversation, your interpretation was merely assumption directly in alignment with your NCB.

Let's think logically about this and use one of my Power Questions: **What are three other ways I can think about this that means nothing about me that would be more empowering?** (1) Maybe she was asking for a feminine product; (2) Maybe she is having an affair and doesn't want everyone to know; (3) Maybe she is getting a promotion and she's not allowed to announce it yet.

Your goal here is to challenge your *perception* of what was going on using logic and removing yourself from the equation. This shift in thinking is a form of a reframe. Consciously reframing your interpretation and thoughts about an event gives your mind options versus looking only at the worst-case scenario. The truth is, we unconsciously tend to take everything personally when most of the time it is *not* about us!

> *"Nothing others do is because of you. What others say and do is a projection of their own reality, their own dream. When you are immune to the opinions and actions of others, you won't be the victim of needless suffering."*

— MIGUEL RUIZ, *THE FOUR AGREEMENTS*

It's crazy that we are so egocentric that we believe that everything revolves around us or involves us. Many times even if someone is directing his or her frustration, judgment, blame or criticism at you, it has nothing to do with you. We don't know what NCB glasses they are wearing that are causing them to react that way.

Another great example of this is road rage. We might get infuriated that a driver *intentionally* cuts us off. Seriously? Nine times out of ten, I bet the other driver wasn't even aware of us at all. Yet your mind assumes that the other driver is driving as they are just to mess with you. Try the Power Question again. Pretend you were cut off in traffic and you're instantly angry. Ask yourself: **What are three other ways I can look at this that means nothing about me that would be more empowering?** (1) I was in their blind spot and they didn't see me; (2) They have kids in the car and were distracted; (3) Their spouse is in the hospital and they are frantically trying to get there.

Once again, all three examples have nothing to do with you. This reframing Power Question is designed to help you think outside the box and give your brain options. There's an old saying that says: *"When we assume, we limit ourselves to one way of thinking when assumptions should be infinite."*

We are lean mean assumption-making machines, constantly filling in the blanks in what we know with a story. To permanently rid yourself of your toxic programs, you must learn to challenge your assumptions. The Power Question will help you do just that. In reality, you will always make assumptions because it's a natural form of thinking. The trick is to not only be *aware* of it but also in *control* of it. By doing so, you can now fill in the blanks with a story that feels more empowering. Here is my golden rule when it comes to making assumptions: ***If you're going to make one (and you will), might as well make one that feels good to you!***

You are still making an assumption, but at least you are making one that will result in having more emotional control. We don't truly know the reasoning behind that driver cutting you off or if it was intentional. And odds are, you will never know. Locking into the belief that you *know* what they are thinking is nothing short of arrogant. Let's challenge these assumptions and *stop taking everything so personally.*

You need to do the same with all the supporting evidence that surrounds your NCB. Many of the stories we have filed in our minds are accompanied by unconscious assumptions. These unconscious assumptions fill our minds with the worst case scenarios. By examining these assumptions we can begin to loosen the grip they have around our NCB.

Processing through trauma and dysfunction is similar. We get to *choose* how to internalize *every* experience. To be clear, I am not saying we should be grateful for being raped, molested, assaulted, abused, or experiencing any other form of trauma. What I am saying is, how you have internalized that experience is having an impact on your overall well-being. Your internal story that has been filed is either building you up or breaking you down. This process of dismantling your supporting evidence is the shift in perspective required for transformation and into healing. The only way to change your NCB is to take away its power—and the supporting evidence is that power.

For me, I found it easier to start shifting my perspective on the smaller wounds like getting kicked out of band and rejected by friends. This gave me practice to tackle the larger issues, the deeper injuries I'd held onto for years or decades. The deeper pains that hurt you the most are pivotal in keeping your NCB in power. As you begin to challenge the supporting evidence of these larger issues, it's not uncommon to get stuck. You may struggle with shifting your perspective at first, and that's okay. When you think about how many years you wore those NCB-colored glasses, it makes sense that you may not be able to see things differently right away. Keep in mind, this process is a journey, one that only *you* can truly understand, so be patient with yourself.

Homework - Dismantling Your Supporting Evidence

Exposing your negative core belief is one of the first steps in reclaiming control over your internal processing systems and becoming more emotionally intelligent.

In this next section, you will work towards reevaluating your supporting evidence. By challenging your perceptions and interpretations logically, you can reclaim the energy held captive by your lingering hurt, anger, guilt, shame, blame or fear. This healing process will start you on the path to total emotional freedom.

Use the exercise you completed in Chapter 3 where you visibly mapped out your NCB and all its supporting evidence. Answer the following questions for each piece of evidence to the best of your ability and with as much detail and insight you can. Keep in mind; your belief system *does not want* to change. It is comfortable in what it knows. Even if your belief system isn't serving you, you know what to expect and, even in your misery, you feel comfortable with it. Push past these limitations and allow yourself to be uncomfortable as you step into the unknown.

- In what ways does this evidence support my NCB? (Connect the dots here.)
- What am I most hurt by, regarding this event/ situation?
- What makes me angry about this?
- Have I forgiven the situation, person or myself? Why or why not?

- What is the benefit of *not* forgiving? (What is the payoff: safety, staying victim, people feeling sorry for me?)
- What am I sacrificing by not forgiving?
- What negative belief system could they have been operating on for them to act/react that way?
- What could have been happening in their life during that time?
- What is a way I could have compassion for them because of this?
- What is something positive I have I learned as a result of this situation? (Resilience, compassion, empathy, independence, strength?)
- How did I grow because of this?
- How has my life benefited because of this positive result?
- If I shifted my perspective, what would it be to? And why?
- How different would my life looked or be with this shift?
- What fears do I have surrounding this shift?
- What would be the worst-case scenario if I adopted this shift?
- How would I benefit?

- What would I lose?
- Do the benefits outweigh the disadvantages?
- If so, what could I do right now to start making the shift? (Think of even just a minor adjustment that could start the process)

CHAPTER 6

Letting Go

"What did I ever do to you God to deserve this life?" I said to myself as I finally escaped the Mississippi mess I was in. I hadn't been able to manipulate the guy I was with like other guys I'd dated. Crying, pleading, guilt tripping—none of my old tactics had any impact on him. He was violent and cruel, threatening to murder me, blowing up my car engine, and beating my head against a wall. After many failed attempts to leave I knew I had to quickly change my tactics if I was ever going to get out alive. I isolated myself from people closest to me, fearful that they might become potential casualties as well. I'm not sure what finally convinced him to let me go, but after more than a year of suffering I was just grateful to be free.

Once safely back in Michigan, I desperately looked for a job. I had burned most of my bridges in the years prior and was left with few options but a good friend finally took me in. After weeks of no employment, I got a lead from an unlikely source, my mother. "John's driver has been sick and he hasn't found a replacement. He's willing to pay you $100 a day if you need money that bad."

I felt I had little choice and reluctantly accepted. It had been years since last I saw him. I was 21 years old and I hoped our relationship would be different. The next day, I drove John to one of his commercial buildings about three hours away. It was a bitterly cold winter day. "We should be home no later than 8 or 9," he told me.

The car ride was uncomfortably quiet for the hours it took to get to his building. Focusing on the road in front of me, I imagined myself being anywhere else but in this moment. I wanted to make myself invisible. We got to the building and he told me to wait in the lobby. "This meeting should only take me about an hour," he said, disappearing in the elevator. I waited in the lobby for hours, silently watching the storm outside gather strength.

It was dark by the time he descended from the elevator. "The roads sure look nasty. I think it's going to be best we stay in the hotel across the street to be safe and I will be sure to pay you an additional $100 for your time," he said. We darted for the car. "Drop me off at the entry and I will go book us rooms. Go park the car and grab my bag from the trunk," he instructed. Fearful of making any waves or causing any trouble I did as I was told.

I followed John to the elevators and up to the floor. He opened the room door for me—then followed me in. "Don't you have your own room?" I asked. "I figured I would just save the money so that I could pass the savings along to you. This way you get an extra $100," he replied.

Every muscle in my body tensed with disgust. *Share a room with him?!* "Is that alright?" he asked as I stood there in silence. Inside, my mind was screaming *"NO! NO! NO BONNIE! DON'T TRUST HIM!"* Paralyzed with fear, I nodded okay. *OKAY!?!? Bonnie, what are you thinking, the answer is NO! 'Get your own room dick head!' That's what you should say! Why can't you stand up to him! Tell him to get lost!"* I jumped on my bed and clicked on the TV, feeling sheer panic throughout my entire body. I felt sick to my stomach and wanted nothing more than for this night to be over. "*Calm down, Bonnie. Just ignore him and pretend to fall asleep quickly. We can get through this and we can really use the extra money,*" I thought.

Before I had a chance to fake falling asleep, his lips pressed against mine and he climbed on top of me. I pushed back and cocked my head towards the side. I began to fight him off me with intensity. I was much stronger and had enough of this abuse. My body was consumed with rage. "Either get off me or I will die trying to get you off me!" I screamed. Startled by my reaction, he left and got his own room.

Alone, I began pacing back and forth in the room. I was seething with anger, hate, disgust and rage. I wanted to hurt him. I wanted him to feel the pain tearing at my heart. I finally calmed down enough to realize the situation I was in. I was hours away from home, without a car, stuck with a person who couldn't drive but controlled the keys, and in the midst of a nasty storm.

Feeling lost, I called my mother. Afraid to admit the truth and cause any more trouble, I minimized the truth and told her I just couldn't drive him anymore. I pleaded with her to come get me. She responded with, "I think you're being overly dramatic Bonnie, you will be fine." Looking back now, I understand why she would say these words knowing nothing of the truth.

But at the time, that was it for me. The last straw. My heart could no longer take the pain and I was ready to check out permanently. My rage had turned to grief, despair and hopelessness. As I laid there, I begged God to end my life. I pleaded with him to take me back home. *"Take me to a place where no one can hurt me again. Take me to place where there is no pain or sorrow."* I just wanted the pain to end.

After soaking the pillow with tears and laying on the bed in grief, I was ready. Ready to meet my Maker. As I removed blades from the razor in the bathroom, I heard my phone ringing in the other room. I ignored it at first, not caring who was calling. I started thinking about my goodbye letter. *"This will teach them,"* I said to myself. *"They will have to live with my death on their hands forever."*

I was jolted out of my thoughts when the phone rang a second time. It was late. Who kept trying to get a hold of me? Didn't they know I'm busy? I ignored the phone again. But when it rang a third time, I couldn't help but answer, "What!" I shouted. Strangely enough, it was an ex-boyfriend who didn't like being ignored. We talked for several minutes and, sensing my despair, he asked me the most unlikely question: "When's the last time you talked to your real father?" Surprised that he even remembered I had a real father, I sat lost within the question.

After I hung up the phone, I started to wonder if my father would help me. I never thought of this as an option. I was his estranged daughter and the last time I'd seen him was very briefly three years before. I felt a tiny glimmer of hope. *"What do I have to lose by asking?"* I scrambled through my phone to find his number and dialed it. As the phone began to ring, I panicked. *"Why would he save you? No one else cares, so why would he? All you would do is mess up like you always do. Just hang up Bonnie, leave him to his peace. His life is better off without you,"* I thought as the answering-machine message finished. Thinking quickly, I left what must have sounded like the most pathetic message ever: "Hey, it's Bonnie. Haven't talked to you in a while and just wanted to call and ask about the weather."

Mortified that I had disturbed someone I barely knew with my troubles, I turned back to my original plan. But a few minutes after leaving my message, the phone again rang. Petrified to see my father's name pop up on my caller ID, I almost didn't answer. I decided in that instant that I would not bother him with my troubles and just talk about the weather. Unbeknownst to me, however, a prophecy was about to be fulfilled that my father had been expecting for over a decade.

We all experience a turning point at one point or another on our life's journey. In this pivotal moment, that often comes when we are at our weakest, our only option is to let go. If we fight and hold on out of fear of loss or lack, our fear blinds us from seeing our greatest path. In my story, I was fully ready to end my own life. In that precise moment, a flicker of hope saved my life. I truly believe that miracles happen every day and that angels can change the course you are on. I didn't remember mentioning anything to my ex about my real father, and never would I have thought of calling my father without his suggestion. Opportunities emerge all around us if we are looking for them. Luckily for me, this opportunity hit me on the head like a ton of bricks, making it impossible to ignore. Even so, fear reared its ugly head, advising me not to disturb my father with my issues.

It's often in our darkest hours with no hope in sight that we finally LET GO. I let go of my fear of not being wanted, or not being enough. I let go of the assumption that he was going to be like everyone else in my life. I let go of my hate of God and the hopelessness that consumed my heart.

I love this quote by Bishop T.D. Jakes: ***"When you hold onto your history, you do so at the expense of*** *your destiny."* You cannot fully embrace your life or experience true transformation if you are unwilling to *let go* of the hurt, sorrow, pain, blame or guilt of the past. You must be willing to experience something different than what you have known. The story surrounding your NCB cannot change unless you are willing to truly shift it. In the last chapter we talked about shifting our perspective. This is a powerful step in the right direction but it is just a stepping stone that leads to the next major leap: forgiveness.

"You cannot fully embrace your life or experience true transformation if you are unwilling to let go of the hurt, sorrow, pain, blame, or guilt of the past."

Forgiveness is the next step on this journey. You must let go of your past through forgiveness long before you can ever think of rebuilding. Forgiveness is your turning point. And not the "Yeah, I forgive them" surface forgiveness. I mean true forgiveness that echoes to the depths of your soul.

Many of my clients claim to have forgiven people in their past when they first come into my office, but they quickly realize how far they still have to go. If your past negatively affects you in any way, including an unwillingness to be vulnerable, lack of trust of others, insecurity or self-doubt (just to name a few), then you have not wholeheartedly let go or forgiven.

Why would anyone want to forgive someone who has wronged them, abused them, or hurt them in the past? Well, Forgiveness is not for the other person or anyone else. It is solely and indisputably for you and you alone. Forgiveness frees you from destructive emotions and allows you to finally step forward, joyfully ready for anything. Think of it as reclaiming your power.

Before we go any further, I do want to make a key point that took me a long time to grasp: *Forgiveness requires you to accept what has happened but this does not mean it makes what happened acceptable.* Accepting *does not* equal acceptable behavior. The goal is to come to terms with your past. Accepting that what happened, happened, and no amount of money, time or energy can change even the slightest bit of it. You can accept what has happened without making it acceptable. Author Joan Borysenko once said in an interview, "You can forgive someone who has wronged you and still call the police and testify in court." Forgiveness does not mean you hang around for future maltreatment or abuse. It is the process of letting go of emotions that weigh you down, not about letting them off the hook. Tony Robbins says it best, *"Forgiveness is a gift you give yourself."* Learning a healthy practice of forgiving is something you do for you so that you can live out the best version of yourself.

As you embark on this journey, you may find it requires you to make hard choices or cut ties with people that do not serve you. During my healing journey, a therapist once told me that my family was toxic to my recovery and encouraged me to cut ties until I was healthy enough to change the dynamics of our relationship. This was some of the hardest, but yet best advice I received at that time.

"Accepting does not equal acceptable behavior!"

Forgiveness goes much deeper than just accepting that the past "is what it is." True acceptance requires you to let go of the toxic and negative feelings that are keeping your NCB stuck. Feelings are the guards that stand watch over the belief, ensuring it will not escape. When you experience pain, suffering, loss, guilt or shame, the body physically hurts from these low-frequency emotions and tends to try to avoid them with any means necessary. We are naturally hardwired to seek pleasure and avoid pain at all cost. So when you have a negative experience, your brain will naturally lock that memory as something it does not want to experience again.

Many of us don't realize that harboring these emotions, not letting go of the past and withholding forgiveness in any shape or form regardless of its intention, is sending out an energy frequency attracting and matching the same frequency to it. Energy attracts like energy—period. If you are holding onto a grudge towards yourself, the world or the people in it, then you will attract and perceive more of what you resist. Even if your intention of holding this belief is to protect you, it is still broadcasting to the world: "This is how I feel. Please bring me more of these people or situations so that I can validate my truth." If you believe that "all men are stupid," you'll attract and notice more men in your life who seem to be stupid. If you think "all women are liars," then you'll attract more situations involving dishonest women. Your belief *has* to validate itself to remain the truth and retain its power. If you shift into wholehearted forgiveness, your negative belief doesn't have a leg to stand on.

Many people feel they've already done enough work on forgiving. I encourage you to go try this process anyway. Forgiveness takes practice and constant repetition, especially if you have held a grudge for a long time. One of the biggest misconceptions about forgiveness is that forgiveness is a feeling. It doesn't always start off that way. Forgiveness is a choice and a choice you may have to make multiple times before it starts generating the feeling of forgiveness. It is not something you can do once and—poof—you're good. It requires time and patience.

Before you begin your homework, I share this thought. I previously mentioned the quote from Omar Khayyam: ***"The moving finger writes and having writ, moves on; nor all your piety nor wit shall lure it back to cancel half a line, nor all your tears blot out a word of it."*** Your past has been written, and no amount of complaining, guilt, shame, crying or anger can change even a millisecond of it. Do not linger in the past. You cannot change what has been done nor what you have done. Learn from your mistakes, learn from the lessons of your past, and move into forgiveness. Never forget: Forgive, learn and grow. Embrace this process and I assure you peace awaits on the other side.

One last thing before you start on your homework, another quote, this one from *The Four Agreements* by Miguel Ruiz:

"God is life. God is life in action. The best way to say, 'I love you, God,' is to live your life doing your best. The best way to say, 'Thank you, God,' is by letting go of the past and living in the present moment, right here and now. Wherever life takes away from you, let it go. When you surrender and let go of the past, you allow yourself to be fully alive in the moment. Letting go of the past means you can enjoy the dream that is happening right now."

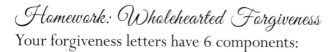

Homework: Wholehearted Forgiveness

Your forgiveness letters have 6 components:

1) Emotional Release
2) Acceptance
3) Reframe
4) Forgive
5) Higher Vision
6) Let Go

Write this as if it is a letter you plan to send to the person or situation you are forgiving. However, *no one will see this letter.* So be 100% honest and let it all out! As you embark on this next stage of healing, you will refer again to the supporting evidence you mapped out in Chapter 3. Write a forgiveness letter to each piece of supporting evidence. Yes, this is going to take you some time and, no, this is not going to be easy. I personally think that is why so many people never choose to change or leave their own needless suffering. It requires a lot of work. No thought can be left unchallenged and, until your new core belief is installed and running on autopilot, it takes a lot of time and energy to maintain your new path.

Begin with:

Dear_____,

Step 1: Emotional Release: In this section, express the authentic, unfiltered, raw thoughts and feelings you harbor towards the situation. Allow yourself to judge, resent, blame, get angry, be hurt, yell, scream or cry on paper. Just get it all out of your system. Your thoughts and feelings do not need to be rational or logical here, so let it flow. This step could take you one page or ten, depending on how much stored emotion needs to be released. If you still feel hurt or angry, keep writing until you get it all out. Example: "I am so hurt that you could be so inconsiderate and such a…"

Step 2: Acceptance: What is your bottom line here? What hurts the most or makes you the angriest?) Example: "I can't trust anyone because of this person." Is there anything you can do to change what has happened? How does holding onto this conclusion negatively affect your life today? In what ways does it benefit you? Example: "It keeps me from trusting others." In what ways can you shift into accepting what has happened? Finally, write out an acceptance statement. Example: "I accept that the past is the past and there is nothing I can do to change what has happened. All I can do is learn and grow from it."

Step 3: Reframe: Power Question: What are three other ways I could look at this that are not about me and would be more empowering?

Step 4: Forgiveness: Write out what and why you choose to forgive. How will you benefit as a result of letting go of this hurt and choosing to forgive?

What does wholehearted forgiveness look like in this situation?

After you complete these questions, shift into feeling forgiveness. Close your eyes and place your hand on your heart. Take slow, deep breaths. Picture the person or situation in your mind, and imagine them surrounded by a bright golden light. Continue your deep, slow breathing, and affirm over and over again: "*I forgive you for your mistake. I release your energy and request the release of mine. I forgive you for your mistake.*" Do this multiple times and choose to feel forgiveness with each breath.

Sincerely,
(Sign Here)

P.S. Step 5: The Higher Vision: In this section, write about how different your life is now that you have forgiven this situation or person. What has changed, what new joys or happiness have you found. What is different about you? Are you lighter, happier, funnier, more open-minded? Be sure to write this out as if it is all true for you right now. You have to actively and repeatedly choose forgiveness. Use statements such as

"I am so grateful now that…" and "my life is so much
_____ now that I have chosen to let go!"

Step 6: Let Go: Now that you have released your
emotions, moved into forgiveness, and mapped out
your higher vision, it is time to let this all go. This
step is your physical release. You can choose to burn
this letter, read it aloud to an empty chair, shred it
or—my personal favorite—mail it to no one without a return label. I have addressed mine to: No One,
1234 Nowhere Rd, Anytown, Away 12345. I even
placed a stamp without a return address and mailed
it! The act of physically letting this go has a dramatic
impact on your psyche.

Rebooting the Subconscious Mind

IN THE LATE 90's, my father left everything he owned and moved to a Native American reservation to study with a Cherokee tribe and learn traditional energy medicine. He hadn't seen his children for almost a decade. After many months, he was approached by the chief during a ceremony who had a premonition. "I have been told that someday one of your children will call and no matter what the circumstances, you must say 'yes.' It will be imperative that you do so." The moment he heard my pathetic voice message about the weather, my father knew this premonition had come to pass.

I picked up the phone on the last ring. My voice was flat and vague. "How's the weather there in Cali?" I muttered, too emotionally exhausted to know what else to say. The conversation dragged for several minutes before my father burst out, "I don't really like pink elephants in the room and can tell you want to ask me something. If the answer to your question is already 'yes,' does it make it easier for you to ask?"

My jaw about hit the floor as I threw myself from the bed. My eyes filled with tears. For a moment, I wondered if I'd only fantasized what he'd just said. His words felt like a miracle out of a *Lifetime* movie, far from the reality I was used to. Completely overwhelmed, I fell to my knees. Doing everything I could to hold myself together, I muttered, "Yes…may…I please move to California?" Within minutes, we planned out the details of my move across the country that was to occur in just a few short days. I felt like I was dreaming.

After hanging up, my emotions stumbled all over themselves. Excitement, pain, fear, and panic pounded in my chest. I lay in bed for the rest of the evening, staring up at the ceiling. *"God, how did he know? Did you do this?"* I asked almost expecting an answer. *"I didn't think you cared about me. I'm so hurt and angry, and feel so lost and empty inside. Why didn't you just let me die? Please help me not fuck this one up too,"* I pleaded.

The next day, I was eager to get back into town. Nothing seemed to faze me. I kept quiet for the remaining drive home. After collecting my $300, I ran off to sort through my remaining belongings.

Packing everything I owned into three duffle bags, I purchased a one-way train ticket to Sacramento. I was beside myself as everything seemed to fall magically into place. A few days before, I'd been desperately lost and alone in a cold hotel room. Now I was beginning my three-day journey across the country with just a few hundred dollars left to my name.

I spent most of the train journey in silence, journaling, listening to music, detoxing, and getting lost in the beauty of the countryside. I had no idea what to expect, or how things were going to be with my father. I had spent so many years hating him and still harbored a lot of bitterness and resentment that he had abandoned me to such a cruel world.

I wasn't prepared for the whirlwind of emotions that hit me when I arrived in California. I got there just in time for my father's birthday party where I was introduced to a slew of his friends. As he paraded me around the room, introducing me to everyone as his daughter, I couldn't help but cringe. *Who does he think he is, talking about how proud he was of me and bragging about me being his daughter? He doesn't even know me and wasn't there,* I thought. Feeling overwhelmed, I called it an early evening and retreated to the motor home which was to serve as my apartment.

As the weeks passed, my emotions started to get the best of me. I was so overwhelmed by the generosity of my father and his girlfriend who welcomed me into their home with open arms. I continued trying to play nice with my family back home, desperately seeking their approval. But they viewed my choice to connect with my father as a betrayal and told me I was exiled from the family. Hearing this news as I stood on top of the motor home (the only place I could get cell service), tears started to stream down my face. I sat up there sobbing and finally I felt my father settling in beside me. He held me as I sobbed, "Nothing I do is ever good enough for them! They blame this on me! Why can't they just love me?!" He tried to comfort me but I was beyond the point where I could hear his words.

In the past, I would use drugs, cigarettes or alcohol to numb my pain but I had given those up on my way to California. I had no idea where to get them in this new land. I felt trapped in my grief, confusion and pain. So, I turned to the only thing available—food. I binged until I went numb, thus starting my three-year struggle with bulimia.

Moving to California was the best thing that could have ever happened to me. I was exposed to things I never dreamed of and healing opportunities I had long given up. But starting on my healing journey opened wounds and emotions that had lain dormant for over a decade. Unable to handle this flood of feeling I was so used to numbing out, I quickly traded one numbing technique for another and another.

After my struggle with bulimia, I became a fitness junkie, then a workaholic. I went from crappy relationship to crappy relationship in search of the acceptance and love I had long felt missing. I finally started to settle down emotionally in my mid-twenties. I made mistakes, got mad, cried, broke down and yet I was relentlessly determined to become a normal functioning member of society.

I plunged forward, taking every class, reading every book, going to rehab, therapy, coaching and going to any seminars I could. With each insight, and each step I grew closer and closer to my goal of being healed. I discovered that my healing path was unique to me and me alone, just as your path of healing will be unique to you. Transformation is not one-size-fits-all technique. It is combination of many lessons over many years that piece the jagged jigsaw puzzle together.

You and I are endangered species! The neural pathways and firing frequencies in your brain are as unique to you as your fingerprint. In fact, the odds that someone else's brain is neurologically identical to yours is mathematically impossible. To transform your unique neural pathways, you'll have to try new things, go new places, talk to new people and be willing to get out of your comfort zone!

Anyone who has risen above dysfunction and trauma can tell you, healing takes time and work. *No one is going to save you!* If you want change, you must be willing to work for it.

Your mind is like a garden. If it is not taken care of, weeded, watered and provided with proper sunlight, it will shrivel up and die. Full transformation requires work. It requires you to weed out your negative, toxic thoughts and beliefs so that the flowers of the mind have a chance to grow. Each garden is different, each weed is different, each environment requires different treatment to ensure the flowers grow. It is up to you to learn your path, to try different approaches with what my father calls "a beginner's mind." Be willing to try new things and new techniques until you find one that fits with your neurological processing system.

And don't give up. Each new skill you learn, whether it feels like it's working or not, is getting you closer and closer to the healing you have been looking for. Truthfully, as we enter into the rebuilding process of this book, it will require you to tend to your garden daily!

"And don't give up. Each new skill you learn, whether it feels like it's working or not, is getting you closer and closer to the healing you have been looking for."

Throughout this book we have examined, explored, dismantled and weakened your NCB and all its supporting evidence. Hopefully, you have felt a shift, a weakening of its power. As you continue to challenge your conscious thoughts and feelings by using your TFA Tracker from Chapter 4, it's time to start the rebuilding process.

The rebuilding process is necessary after the process we used to dismantle your NCB. We have to install a new program. It might sound like one of these: "Who I am is good enough." "I am loved and supported by all those around me and I see this now." "I can trust the people I love including myself and I know this now." "My life is filled with joy and purpose and I feel this now." These are all great positive core beliefs. Either choose one that suits your belief system or create a new one. Make sure this power statement (a.k.a. affirmation) speaks to your soul and directly opposes your original NCB.

If your negative core belief was "I am not worthy," then I'd recommend "I am worthy and feel it now!" Add "I feel it (see it, hear it, know it) now" after your power statement. Choose one that best fits your learning style. For example, if you are an auditory learner, use "I hear this now." Using words that engage your senses will help optimize your power statement.

After you have created the new program you wish to lock into your subconscious mind, it is time to start gathering the support needed to bolt it into place. To do this, look back into your past to uncover positive pivotal moments you experienced. If you have only reminisced about the painful memories and anything good that ever happened for most of your life, this might be tricky at first. Initially, I had the same difficulty.

Remember that the brain has a negative bias. Our brain recalls and retains a negative experience over a positive one as a means of protecting itself. If I burned myself touching a hot stove, I would want my brain to quickly recall this memory so that I avoid hot stoves without hesitation. Similarly, if someone hurts my feelings, this negative bias may retain this memory as "I can't trust anyone." Struggling to distinguish between perceived threats and actual threats, this negative brain bias can work against us.

If someone hurts you, of course you should be cautious around them. However it is distorted to think *all* people will be hurtful. This is where we need to apply our logical thinking. Is it logical that everyone in the world is capable of making this exact same mistake and hurting you? Despite what you may feel, the logical conclusion is "no." No two people on this earth are neurologically wired and fire in the same way. Many people may have the same response or reaction but it is not logical to think *everyone* in the world is the same.

"Many people may have the same response or reaction but it is not logical to think everyone in the world is the same."

Here is a tip that helped me make this shift: "Stop punishing others for someone else's mistake." Not everyone in the world is a liar, manipulative, conniving or ill-tempered. Some people are, but as you continue to shift your perspective you won't be looking for that type of person any longer to validate your old beliefs.

"Stop punishing others for someone else's mistake."

When I moved from state to state, my troubles followed me. Why? Because my belief systems followed me. I had to shift my perspective and transform my belief system to start meeting functional, healthy, loving individuals. Today my life is filled with some of the most outstanding, loving and supportive people you'll find on this planet. I would never have been able to see them or felt worthy enough to be loved by them if I hadn't shifted my belief system and started looking for people that matched up with this new belief that I was worthy.

As you begin to rebuild, you will do so in two parts: the past and the present. Memories from the past have weight to them and can help lock in the new belief faster, but gathering evidence in the now is just as important. I lived through a traumatic childhood, but not every moment was awful. I doubt that every moment of *your* past was 100% horrible either. I bet with enough thought and exploration, you too can find quite a bit of joy in your past. Maybe it wasn't from home, but rather from the friends you had, a teacher, school, or a grandparent. Positive pivotal moments are uplifting times that have empowered you along the way. These moments could be something monumental or as simple as winning first place in your elementary talent show.

When your NCB was running the show, these positive experiences might have been overlooked or given very little recognition. These mini-victories, successes or empowering moments can help to dramatically strengthen your new core belief and shape a new outlook on love, life, family, self or even how you trust. You can strengthen your new belief further by fueling it with feelings of love, joy, passion, courage, accomplishment, confidence, etc. By exploring these pivotal moments, we can clearly define thoughts and feelings that reinforce, empower and embed your new core belief deeply into your subconscious mind.

Discovering my positive pivotal moments was a huge shift for me. So accustomed to telling my victim story, I never stopped to think of any joy I had experienced. My victim story kept me stuck feeling sorry for myself and kept others feeling sorry for me.

This energy attracted more people and situations that matched its frequency of suffering and lack. The more I told my story and dismissed any thought of a positive past, the more I became disempowered. In the beginning I felt my story defined me and without it, I was nothing. I had to learn to tell a new story that empowered me.

In the homework below, you'll explore your positive pivotal moments in yearly increments just as you did for your NCB while simultaneously gathering evidence in the present. The conscious and the subconscious work together in synchronicity. For true transformation we have to not only change our hidden subconscious thoughts, we have to change the surface level ones as well.

Your first major win will come as you learn to stop blaming and complaining. Stop complaining about how bad you had it or how much they hurt you. Stop blaming your past for your troubles you have today. Stop blaming another person for your behavior, actions or reactions. For change to occur, you have to take 100% personal responsibility for your thoughts, feelings, actions and reactions. Taking responsibility of your change does not mean shaming or taking ownership of how others acted or reacted.

Your past isn't your fault. But what you choose to do with today it is entirely up to you. You do not have to be victim to what was—you can *choose* something different.

To change the present, you use the TFA tracker you learned earlier. Be mindful of your thoughts and feelings. Are they serving you or weakening you? Mindfulness of your thinking will serve as your anti-virus software and protect your mind from future viruses. Without your *conscious* efforts, your subconscious reprogramming will never have a chance. Consciously gather evidence throughout your day that supports your new belief. If someone buys you a coffee, use it as validating evidence. If you get a compliment: Validation! If you get a promotion, award or acknowledgement: Validation! If your spouse buys you flowers, takes you on a date, or even takes out the trash: Validation! If your kids draw you a picture or tell you how much they love you: Validation!

Make it your goal to celebrate *all* your wins. Gathering evidence will help you do just that. Take a picture, write a note or find a picture to commemorate the positive moment. Place it in a gratitude jar or journal,

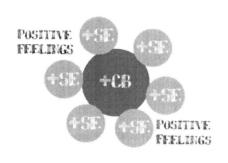

or hang it on your vision board. Post it on what my husband, calls a Victory Board. This is a board where you display all your victories, certificates, pictures and accomplishments. Hang it where you can see it or visit it daily.

Find whatever fits your lifestyle best and start. We have so many options of vision boards, both physical and digital, so no excuses! Take this time to stop the crazy cycle and fearlessly embrace the unknown. If transformation is what you really want, work for it. It takes 18-21 days to build a habit. If you do not work at it daily and remind yourself daily, your old beliefs, habits and behaviors step back in. Be willing to see, feel and choose differently.

So now that you are actively working with your subconscious, let's explore those past positive pivotal moments to lock this new belief in!

Homework: Positive Pivotal Moments

Part 1: In Chapter 3, visually mapping your NCB helped you clearly see how your life has been affected or limited. Let's use the same process to help you visually map your new belief as we search for supporting evidence.

Use the diagram below as a reference. In the center, place your new Positive Core Belief (PCB). The larger circles surrounding your PCB will represent different eras of your life. Make circles for ages 1-5, 6-10, 10-15, 15-20, 20-25, 25-30, 30-40, 40-50, and 50+. In each circle, recall a memory, friend, accomplishment, joy, or experience that supports your new PCB.

Did you date anyone during that time, have a nice vacation, have a pet, get a promotion, win anything, buy a new car, go to a concert or show, have fun with a friend, have a child, get married, or have a fun birthday? Look back on your social media timeline and see what positive events took place! If nothing comes up, jog your memory by meditating or listening to music you listened to at that time in your life. If more than one thing comes up, write it down! Recall as many memories as you can to help strengthen your new belief.

Part 2: Journaling exercise. Reflecting on each positive pivotal moment, ask yourself the following questions:

- Why was this event, person or situation so uplifting?
- How did I feel?
- What hidden strengths or personal gifts did I use to help make it possible?
- What did I learn from it?
- In what ways did it help me grow?
- What lesson can I take from this today with my new perspective?
- How does this memory support my new belief?
- What aspect of this event can I use for supporting evidence?

CHAPTER 8

Victim to Victory: A Story Retold

LIKE MANY PEOPLE today, I came from a broken home filled with dysfunction and chaos. Family fighting, sexual abuse, abandonment and emotional detachment lead me down a path of self-destruction. With each bad decision and failure my belief of worthlessness was amplified which only made things worse. Unknown to me, this feeling of worthlessness was the catalyst that would haunt my life, thoughts, happiness and decisions for more than a decade.

It was in my darkest hour — when the walls caved in around me, people turned against me and predators took advantage of me — that I felt I had reached my end. I could go no further and could take no more. It was the smallest flicker of fate and an abrupt move to California that saved my life during this bleak time.

With the opportunity to safely explore change, I began to untangle a lifetime of dysfunction. I forced myself to take a long, hard look in the mirror, and declared, "It is time to take responsibility for your life and learn to love you!" From that point on, I vowed to learn how to respect myself, release my internal blocks, and break free into a life filled with more joy, love, purpose, and fulfillment than I could have ever imagined. But healing didn't happen overnight. I didn't just wake up one day and find myself magically healed. It took work and lots of it. In fact, it took my relentless desire and unwavering faith to finally reach the other side.

Today however, I look back with deep empathy for the pain that little girl endured, and passionately value the strength it gave me to be the woman I am today. If it wasn't for all the hardship, I know I wouldn't be able to help others like me transform their lives. Looking back now, I understand that the heartache and pain I suffered was neither intentional nor personal. Understanding, empathy and compassion floods my heart as I embrace those around me, accepting their imperfections and acknowledging that they are victims of their own suffering as well. My story empowers me to do good within this world and it has sent me on a healing journey that I would not trade for anything. I thank my past for the freedom I have today.

WOW, right? What a shift from the story you have been reading all along. In this rewritten story, I acknowledged my past struggle (without going into major details), then pivoted it towards the greatest lessons and blessings. This is called a victim-to-victory rewrite and is the next step in your transformation. For many years you have told your story, gathered sympathizers, supporters and defenders. But now it's time to change your tune. I unconsciously cast myself as the victim in my story believing that if you felt sorry for me, then you would protect me and wouldn't hurt me. As the victim, I desperately needed heroes to "save" me. How I told my story attracted rescuers who were unconsciously looking for someone to save. This victimhood was a survival technique that was entrenched deep within my belief system, just like yours is doing for you.

How we each tell our story or why we bury it deep isn't without reason. Ask yourself, what is your reason? What role do you use it for? Are you the rescuer, the victim, the martyr, the persecutor, the orphan, the people-pleaser, the rebel or the jester? Pause for a moment and think about this.

Through our experiences we are conditioned to play the roll of one or more of these characters. A great example of this is within every classic Disney princess movie. Have you ever noticed there are 3 main characters; the hero, the victim and the villain. Many times the victim turns into the hero in the end, however they have to reach a breaking point before the transformation occurs. The victim is either res-cued by the hero and lives happily ever after, or the victim is forced to be the hero to save themselves. Either way, when you look at the story from a bird's eye view, you can clearly define the roles.

In order to successfully rewrite your own story, it is essential to understand why you tell it in the first place. What is your motivation? This is what I call, "knowing your game." The game is how we play life and what roles we assume in order to win. Every action or move we make has a payoff or benefit. The benefit doesn't always have to be positive. Many peo-ple feel they deserve to be punished so their payoff is getting what they deserve. When you say or do something that is out of alignment with your highest self, question it. Ask yourself: Why am I doing this? What do I have to gain? Maybe your answer is to fit in, feel accepted, people-please, protect yourself or to fill an awkward silence. By questioning your actions, you at least give yourself the opportunity to continue that behavior or alter it to one that serves you better. Without questioning your own words and deeds, you will continue to live a life that is unconscious and out of control, attracting more and more of the things you don't want in your life.

"Every action or move we make has a payoff or benefit."

The way in which you are telling or not telling your story is attracting equivalent energy to it. As I have mentioned countless times in this book, energy attracts like energy. As the old saying goes, "What you resist persists." Every thought and every feeling (which has even more power to it) attracts its equal counterpart. Science has proven this theory, movies have been produced about it, and millions of personal growth books have been written around the power of your thoughts and feelings.

If you talk about, complain about, feel sorry for, blame, persecute, justify or even obsessively think about something, you are opening your life to more and more of that frequency. This is largely because you will only see what you want to see. Remember the brain filters through 400 billion bits of information per second but only processes 2,000 bits of it. So that means that if you are standing in a room looking at 10 potential people to talk to (or even date), your energy will naturally be attracted only to the one or two that best fit your belief system. You might not even notice the other eight people in the room. It's not that they are not there. It's just that the mind filters out the unfamiliar and is naturally drawn towards the familiar. It will lead you where it feels you best fit in or are most comfortable. By rewriting your story, along with all the other tools you learned in this book, you have the opportunity to change your belief system and start to notice the other eight people in the room.

There is one final point to remember before you get started rewriting your story and that is to have compassion for yourself. We tend to judge ourselves so cruelly and harshly for the mistakes that we have made. The judgments and criticism that flow through our minds are so cruel that we wouldn't dare place them upon another soul. Yet, they go unchallenged in our minds. As you are rewriting your letter, many of these judgments and criticisms might emerge.

"The judgments and criticism that flow through our minds are so cruel that we

**wouldn't dare place them upon
another soul."**

One of the biggest areas that I judged myself surrounding the molestation encounters with John was "I should have known better, especially the older I got." These cold, harsh words were locked in my old story tighter than Fort Knox. Having self-compassion means talking to and treating yourself with the same amount of love and respect you would give to a stranger. If a 14-year-old girl came up to me and said "I should have known better than to be molested," would I ever blame or shame her? NO WAY! I would demonstrate compassion, understanding and empathy for her. I would embrace her and encourage her that this was not her fault. Yet, when the tables are turned, I judged and condemned myself for my juvenile behavior. Keep this in mind as you rewrite your story. Ask yourself where you can demonstrate more self-compassion. The easiest way to do this is to ask yourself, "If a friend told me this, what kind and encouraging words would I express to them?"

Let's get started.

Homework: Rewrite your story from Victim to Victory—A shift in reality

In this final assignment, it is time to rewrite your story in a way that uplifts and empowers you while still acknowledging the struggle you went through. It should be no longer than one page long, so choose your words wisely. Though my story may appear to be multiple pages long in this little book, it is only one page on my computer with size 14 font with single spacing. It may take you multiple drafts before you are able to get it just right. I would start by writing an outline listing out the key points that you would want to make in your story. "What pivotal stories are necessary, what lessons did you learn and how has your life benefited because of it?" are just a few questions you might ask yourself.

Once you get your final draft completed, call a friend or family member who has earned your emotional trust and read it to them. Ask them to tell you how it made them feel afterwards, then make any adjustments necessary. The story should leave them feeling inspired, uplifted, motivated or grateful. Once finished, feel free to connect with me on social media or submit and share your new redefined story with our tribe at www.TrueToYourCore.com. I would love to hear from you! Okay friend, get started! I look forward to seeing your new story and all the grateful lessons and strengths it has taught you!

CHAPTER 9

Moving Forward

ONE OF THE most helpful steps in your healing journey is to get out there and connect with a community. You cannot do this alone. You need a tribe. People are your reflections. Without them, you would stay oblivious and blind to your own inner turmoil. Community is essential for your overall health and well-being. It is important to find friends and a community of like-minded people with whom you share similar values and beliefs.

I think there is a lot to be said for the old sayings "You are who you hang out with" and "Misery loves company." You want to surround yourself with people who build you up while still keeping it real, who encourage you and challenge you without harshly criticizing or putting you down. Build a team of people to surround you who are experts in their own unique way. Maybe one is an excellent listener, while another is great at giving good advice. These are the people you have at your round table, friends and trusted advisors.

"But Bonnie, I don't have any friends and it's hard for me to make any." I hear this all the time, and totally understand where you're coming from. But as Henry Ford said, *"Whether you think you can or can't, either way you're right."* Making new friends and finding the right tribe might seem difficult, but it's worth it. Finding new friends is like panning for gold. Sometimes you go out and get nothing, sometimes you find a nugget only to discover it was fool's gold, but once in a great while you get lucky. Those precious nuggets make all the searching worth it.

Building a team of friends starts with being the type of friend you wish to have. Gandhi said: "Be the change you wish to see." I say: Be the friend you wish to have! Stop waiting for friendship to happen and create what you want!

When I first started building my community, I made the mistake of expecting other people to create the friendships I wanted. In reality, friendships take time and effort to build. Instead of complaining that they never called me, I learned to call them. Instead of feeling sad that I was never invited to events, I started creating events to invite others to. I started *being* the friend I wanted to have. The more I did this, the stronger my friendships became. In some cases, people were put off by the close bond I wanted and they rejected me. This didn't mean there was anything wrong with me or with them for that matter. I was just asking for a level of friendship they were not prepared for. No matter what my NCB or even the gossip was trying to say, it was not personal.

"Be the friend you wish to have! Stop waiting for it to happen and create what you want!"

People suffering with depression need community more than anything. Therapists advise them to get moving, get outside and get involved. Once you feel like you belong to something or someone, it is impossible to feel alone. Most people suffering from depression are suffering from guilt, shame and hopelessness. We've all done things, said things and messed things up. Life is messy. We all get "dirty" but that "dirt" can give us strength and character if we let it. Your dirt can either build you up or break you down and this is solely up to you. Throughout this book, I have shared much of my dirt with you and I had even more that didn't make the cut. My life was messy—and I was the biggest mess in it!

For years I blamed myself, punished myself and tore myself down. By doing so, I continued to fuel my NCB, negative thoughts, feelings of grief, sorrow, shame and actions of self-hatred, depression and suffering. I always waited, prayed and dreamed about a prince swooping in, dashing me off my feet and saving me. This fantasy isn't real. You know that story of a damsel in distress who is rescued by her Prince Charming and they ride off into the sunset to live happily ever after? In real life, if the damsel doesn't learn to change her ways, she will quickly find herself in a similar mess over and over again. My father was the knight in shining armor who saved me from the hell I'd created. Yet this save was only temporary. I didn't wake up in California living happily ever after. He showed me the door and I had to choose to walk through it. Trust me, it was a long bumpy road. It wasn't until I cleaned up the mess festering inside me that I found my happily ever after.

"In real life, if the damsel doesn't learn to change her ways, she will quickly find herself in a similar mess over and over again."

Once I cleared my internal mess and transformed my life, the people, places and things around me transformed as well. But change means doing the things you really don't want to do so that you can get different results. Doing the same thing every day expecting a different outcome is literally insanity. I had to *choose* to release my need to be saved and take personal responsibility for saving myself. I had to *choose* to make my life different. I had to *choose* to get out of bed when all I wanted was to pull the covers over my head and hide, I had to *choose* to be around people when I felt like being alone. I had to *choose* to seek help even when I felt there was no hope. It was this courage, this tenacity that saved my life. You have this capacity within you as well. You can *choose* to make your life better.

A different outcome requires a deep look into yourself, your perspectives and your beliefs. Without shining some light on these areas, they will continue to lurk in the shadows, inflicting pain at every opportunity. *Wanting* something more or different is just the first step. *Doing* something to get it is the next.

Fear is the enemy of change and the fuel for ignorance. Don't let fear of failure or rejection stop you from making this change. Change can be painful. It doesn't have to be, but in many cases it will be. The loss of a loved one, breakup, job change, letting go of the past, forgiveness—all can be painful to move through. A shift in perspective and a quick reframe can save you from needless suffering, turning searing pain into minor discomforts. In Buddhism there is a saying "Pain is enviable, suffering is optional." We choose suffering because often we feel it is easier than the alternative when really it's not.

"Fear is the enemy of change and the fuel for ignorance."

Emotion is a natural part of our life and allows us to feel tremendous joy, love and passion. Without it, we would experience life as monotone and dull. Color makes this life vibrant. Emotions allow us to experience it with exhilaration. But the crayon box doesn't only have vibrant colors. It also has dark, earth tones. These darker-toned emotions give us the balance and help us ground our energy.

When we are happy and full of life, we get a sense of being high on life. We are filled with energy and excitement. When we experience sadness, grief, guilt and shame, our energy is low and heavy. But without knowing this low, how could we ever appreciate the highs? The lows balance us out and allow us to deeply appreciate when we experience the highs.

Healthy emotions guide us. Feeling ashamed when you harmed another isn't a bad thing. In fact, it's healthy. The difference between healthy and unhealthy shame is how you choose to perceive your mistake. It's the difference between saying "I did something I am not proud of" versus saying "I am pathetic" or "I am a bad person." The first emphasizes the mistake or situation whereas the latter sets *you* up as the mistake. It is healthy to acknowledge when you have messed up or have done something you are not proud of. It's not healthy to accuse yourself of being the mistake, failure, weak or pathetic. Making a mistake does not mean you are a mistake!

"Making a mistake does not mean you are a mistake!"

Our society today is addicted to being happy. How to be happy books, videos, podcasts, movies, and magazines flood the market. We gobble them up hoping the latest quick fix is the answer. We are obsessed with thinking we need more good and are convinced that something is wrong with us if we experience any negative emotion.

The United States is the most heavily medicated country in the world, and one of the most prevalent prescriptions is antidepressants. For many people, these medications are unnecessarily prescribed. Too many have adopted antidepressants as the quick fix answer to any negativity. I have nothing against medication. For some people, it can be necessary. But for most of us, it is not the final solution! I have helped clients who have been on antidepressants for over a decade. Working together, with their doctor's permission, we are finally able to get them off their medications.

We are addicted to a get-fixed-quick mentality. I believe this is largely because we have value and have prioritized getting whatever we can as quickly as we can, from service to information to food.

With all the fast food, drive-through's, high-speed internet, on-demand television, instant banking, instant mail, instant movies, instant prescription pick-up and non-stop social feeds, we have become obsessed with getting everything instantly. We apply this same mentality to our health. For physical health, you can have 10-minute power workouts, quick fix dieting tools and techniques pushing extremes. For emotional health, you see prescriptions being handed out like breath mints. Mentally, we are bombarded with instant information through TV, high-speed internet and on-demand, oh my!

We've lost our ability to be patient. In fact, if the drive-through takes more than a few minutes, we get frustrated, annoyed and demand an explanation. If our internet is running slow, we have meltdowns. We forget what it was like to have dial-up or no internet at all. We have become so accustomed to getting *what* we want *when* we want it that we have lost the perspective that some things just take time.

Transforming your thoughts and belief systems is a process that takes time. No medication or get-healed-quick technique will get you there. It will require time, work and, in most cases, help.

My complete transformation took me years, many teachers, thousands of hours and tens of thousands of dollars to get where I am today. Some tools and techniques worked better than others. Some teachers had a greater impact on me than others. No one thing got me here. You'll likely require a combination of teachings and tools to spark unique epiphanies within you and move you along your path. Each step brings us a new level of awareness that could not have come before. Rereading a book I had read 10 years ago brought me a level of insight I was not capable of comprehending the first time. It was the same book, yet the words spoke a different meaning to me.

Begin to explore the teaching and lessons this life has to offer. Invest in yourself. You have access to a bounty of information at any given time. Be open-minded, yet be discerning as well. Not everything you read, hear or watch is true, but you can find great help, guidance and support.

As you continue your journey forward, I encourage you to continue using the tools you learned within this book. Don't be afraid to ask for help. Guidance is a gift waiting for action to be applied. Build a community and friendships that support your higher self. Most importantly, be patient and have compassion for yourself. Change takes time.

"Guidance is a gift waiting for action to be applied."

*Be Sure To Check Out Our **Free** Video Master Series That Accompanies The Homework Outlined In This Book At: www.TrueToYour-Core.com*

What's next?

You read this book, did the homework and applied the techniques. Where do you go next? It all depends on what you think you need. Your healing journey will be unique to you. You'll need a combination of resources to help you truly transform. If you find yourself ready, scratch that yearning for more and come join me and the thousands of others who have done the work to change their lives.

After more than a decade of self-exploration, research, training, coaching and teaching, I have created a three-month program designed solely for people who truly want transformation. I call it Emotional Resilience Training. As a fair warning, this program is not meant for people who think they *might* want to change or for people who think change would be nice. No! This program is for people who are committed, determined and *starving* for it.

During our training you will learn to *know* that who you are is good enough. You will become confident, self-aware, emotionally intelligent and self-reliant. It requires work. This course is for the people I call "graduates of therapy." People who have done some work on themselves, who have some insight but still find themselves falling short of their maximum potential. During the 3 months, you have the opportunity to detangle your inner-core belief systems and dig deep within the subconscious mind with homework, tools and exercises. I created a workbook that is over 100 pages long to guide you through this process and help you get out of your way, and on with your life.

Basically, I designed this course for people like me, who want answers. Who want action and are willing to do whatever it takes to get it. If this sounds like you, join us. If this scared you, let us help hold your hand, because I truly believe you are much stronger than you think you are. The journey to self-love and healing is a long one with many ups and downs and you don't have to go it alone. Check it out at www. BonnieKelly.me

Whether you choose to join us now or in the future, I believe in you, my friend. You can have a great life. In-fact, you deserve one! I hope you find the courage to take action and invest in yourself. I have read thousands of self-help books and gained *tons* of insight from them. But I noticed that I could hide behind a book. Change stayed just an idea. Evolution can't happen without action. It's time to become the positive force of change in your life and begin taking active action towards positive growth.

I believe in you. Do you?

With much love and a grateful heart, thank you for sharing this journey with me.

Your Friend,
Bonnie Kelly

_PS:_ I encourage you if you haven't already, go to www. TrueToYourCore.com and claim your **Free Master Video** Series that follows along with this book. It's absolutely free and is designed to help you master the methodologies outlined in this book.

I have designed it in a way for you, your book club, or accountability group to dive deep into the exercises and emerge victories! I highly recommend hosting a mastermind with this book and fostering discussions on how your subconscious programs are wreaking havoc in your lives. True healing steams from discussion. So be brave and dive deep!

Included in our Free Master Video Series you will find downloadable worksheets and discussion questions to help your group get the most out of this program. Wishing you the best of luck!! XOXO

39934129R00090

Made in the USA
San Bernardino, CA
06 October 2016